For all those who want to learn Russian
seriously and with enthusiasm.

© 2024 Self-taught Russian

russian@self-taught-languages.com

Autor:
Nikita Kuznetsov
& Andrey Bernhart

Publisher:
Self-taught Languages
represented by
Andrey Bernhart
Bahnhofstrasse 17
6824 Schlins
Austria

ISBN:
979-8-300-14944-4

Table of contents

1

Introduction

2

Vocabulary section

3

Flashcards

Page 210

Russian	Transliteration	Pronunciation Example
А а	A	"A" as in "car"
Б б	B	"B" as in "bat"
В в	V	"V" as in "van"
Г г	G	"G" as in "go"
Д д	D	"D" as in "dog"
Е е	E	"Ye" as in "yes"
Ё ё	Yo	"Yo" as in "yawn"
Ж ж	Zh	"Zh" as in "treasure" or "pleasure"
З з	Z	"Z" as in "zebra"
И и	I	"Ee" as in "see"
Й й	Y	"Y" as in "boy"
К к	K	"K" as in "kite"
Л л	L	"L" as in "lamp"
М м	M	"M" as in "man"
Н н	N	"N" as in "net"
О о	O	"O" as in "more" (stressed), or "A" as in "car" (unstressed)
П п	P	"P" as in "pen"

Russian	Transliteration	Pronunciation Example
Р р	R	Rolled "R" as in **r**ock (but more rolled)
С с	S	"S" as in "**s**un"
Т т	T	"T" as in "**t**op"
У у	U	"Oo" as in "m**oo**n"
Ф ф	F	"F" as in "**f**un"
Х х	Kh	"H" as in the Scottish "lo**ch**"
Ц ц	Ts	"Ts" as in "ca**ts**"
Ч ч	Ch	"Ch" as in "**ch**at"
Ш ш	Sh	"Sh" as in "**sh**op"
Щ щ	Shch	Softer "Shch," like in "fre**sh ch**eese"
Ъ ъ	Hard sign	No sound; separates hard syllables
Ы ы	Y	A deep "i," as in "**i**ll," but darker
Ь ь	Soft sign	No sound; softens the preceding letter
Э э	E	"E" as in "m**e**t"
Ю ю	Yu	"Yu" as in "**u**niverse"
Я я	Ya	"Ya" as in "**ya**rd"

Introduction

The benefits of language learning

Whether for business or private reasons. Russia is one of the most fascinating countries in the world. And its language is just as captivating.

Russian is not only a beautiful language, it also broadens your horizons enormously.

It is a big step to learn a language that is so different from ours. By understanding the Russian alphabet and Russian vocabulary, you also develop a cultural understanding.

Visiting Russia with or without knowledge of the language are two completely different experiences. The way sentences are formed, words are used and conversations are conducted is completely different to the way we speak English.

So no matter what your personal intention behind learning Russian is, it will definitely be an exciting journey and one that will show you a whole new side of our world.

That's why I love learning new languages so much. Apart from the really useful consequences, such as new business opportunities or making and maintaining friendships across language barriers, simply knowing a completely new language takes you further in every area of life.

Neurologists and linguists have jointly discovered that completely new areas of the brain are activated when you speak another language. This effect even increases the more foreign languages you speak. Learning languages is therefore also seen as one of the most effective methods of preventing old-age dementia and other cognitive diseases in old age.

But let's start with Russian. On the following pages, I present my learning plan, which I will give you so that you can learn Russian as effectively as possible. It is not a rigid template, but more of a guide. Whether you stay on the path or deviate from it is entirely up to you.

The 4-step Russian Learning Guide

1. Learn the Russian Cyrillic alphabet

Unlike the usual languages that native English speakers learn, Russian has a different alphabet. Instead of using the Latin alphabet like Spanish, French, German or many other languages like us, Russian, like Serbian and Bulgarian, uses the Cyrillic alphabet.

In languages with the Latin alphabet, such as Spanish, we can start practicing vocabulary straight away. It is not unusual to have already learned and be able to use the first 10 words on the first day. This is different with Russian.

The first 1-2 weeks are usually completely focused on learning the Russian Cyrillic alphabet. This means that you learn the 33 letters of this new alphabet until you understand and can read them all by heart.

Only then does it really make sense to practise vocabulary and grammar. Otherwise, you won't be able to read the writing and will always have to rely on transcriptions, which is not very beneficial for learning. You will also find these transcriptions in our book, but only in the vocabulary section and not on the flashcards. You will find them in the vocabulary section because they emphasize the stress of the word again. Russian words also change depending on the stress. As this is not normally apparent in the writing itself, but has to be memorized, we have marked each stress in the transcribed version with a ' above the respective letter. But more on this later.

There are many ways to learn the Cyrillic alphabet. The most effective way, as in this book, is to use flashcards. You can find lots of learning material online to learn Cyrillic quickly.

If you want an app for learning and also writing exercises so that you can not only read the script but also write it directly, then I recommend my first Russian textbook: The Russian Workbook. It will teach you the correct pronunciation, how to read Cyrillic and how to write it.

You can go directly to the book on Amazon here.

2. Learn Your First 720 Russian Words

Now that you have mastered the alphabet, you have many options for how to proceed.

The two main options are grammar and vocabulary. Grammar consists of various conjunctions and verb forms, adjective intensification, sentence structure and much more. Here you will learn the theory behind the language. How things work, why sentences are formed the way they are and much more. If you are a grammar nerd, you can also learn grammar directly in the second step. It's not necessarily my recommendation, but it's definitely possible.

What I do recommend is learning vocabulary. As quickly as possible, as much as possible. According to linguists, the most effective way to learn a language and to be able to retain and use what you have learned is to learn vocabulary.

Sentence structure and grammar are extremely important, but simply learning vocabulary is still much more effective. In many conversations, you will understand more and more fragments and eventually whole sentences, simply because you have acquired a vocabulary.

It's also much more fun to learn grammar with a vocabulary. Every grammar rule you learn expands your vocabulary again indirectly through the many word forms and possible uses of your vocabulary.

This book focuses on exactly that: teaching you all 720 A1 vocabulary words as quickly as possible. More specifically, this book does not give you an exact pace. I will make recommendations later on how many words you should learn, but it largely depends on your motivation and how much time you can invest in learning each day. Think of this book like a sports car. If you want to drive very fast, this book will allow you to do so. But if you want to drive slowly at your own pace, then you can do that with this book too.

3. Learn all the important rules of grammar

The Russian sentence structure is different from ours. For example, there is no article like "the." Instead, the noun is simply named without an article. Additionally, Russian relies heavily on grammatical cases, which means that the endings of nouns, pronouns, and adjectives change depending on their function in the sentence. This can be a significant adjustment for English speakers, who rely more on word order and helper words to indicate meaning.

In Russian, the concept of grammatical cases is one of the core elements of sentence construction. These cases define the role of each word in a sentence, whether it acts as the subject, an object, or shows possession or direction. Instead of using prepositions or fixed sentence positions to clarify meaning, Russian uses these changes in word endings, which gives the language much more flexibility in word order.

Another unique aspect of Russian grammar is its verb system. Russian verbs are categorized into two aspects: one indicating incomplete or ongoing actions, and the other for completed actions. This means that the same verb can take on different forms depending on whether the action is viewed as ongoing or finished, adding a layer of precision and nuance to expressing time and intention.

Furthermore, sentence structure in Russian is far more flexible than in English. While English relies on a strict word order to convey meaning, Russian allows words to move around within a sentence to emphasize different parts. This is possible because grammatical cases ensure that the meaning remains clear, regardless of the word order.

Learning to understand and navigate these elements—cases, verb aspects, and flexible sentence construction—is an important step in grasping Russian grammar. At this stage, it is not about mastering every detail but becoming aware of how the language functions differently from English and gradually familiarizing oneself with these new concepts. This foundation will make it easier to interpret written and spoken Russian and begin forming sentences with confidence.

I explicitly recommend learning grammar only once you have a basic vocabulary. You don't have to know all the words in this book, but you should know at least a third of them before you start studying grammar rules. My learning strategy emphasizes focus and sequence because this has proven to be the most effective way to not only learn a language quickly, but also to stay motivated. The biggest problem with language learning is that many people stop early because they lack such a clear plan. If you stick to my clear sequence, it will be much easier for you to stay motivated and get closer to your goal every day.

4. Practicing conversations in everyday life

After you have understood the basics of grammar and sentence structure, there comes a "magic moment," as I like to call it. From now on, you will understand whole Russian sentences—at least simple Russian sentences. This gives you completely new opportunities to continue learning.

At this stage, the focus shifts from learning isolated words and grammatical rules to recognizing patterns and building a deeper connection with the language. You will start to see how verbs, nouns, and adjectives interact within sentences, how cases dictate their roles, and how word order subtly changes the emphasis or meaning. This is when Russian begins to feel less like a set of rules and more like a living, breathing system of communication.

One of the most exciting parts of this stage is being able to read and understand simple texts. Whether it's short stories, dialogues, or even basic news headlines, you'll find yourself picking out familiar words and phrases, gradually piecing together the meaning of sentences. Each successful moment of comprehension will boost your confidence and motivate you to tackle more complex material. Moreover, this is the time to expand your vocabulary in context. Instead of memorizing individual words, you'll encounter them in phrases and sentences, learning not only their meanings but also how they are used naturally by native speakers. This will help you internalize not just the words themselves but their grammatical forms and typical collocations. You'll also start to experience the rhythm and flow of the language. Listening to Russian will become easier, as you'll recognize sentence structures and anticipate what comes next. Speaking will feel more intuitive, as you combine familiar words and phrases into your own sentences. This is when the language truly starts to come alive, and your learning process becomes more dynamic and rewarding.

At this point, learning becomes about active engagement with the language. Whether through reading, listening, or practicing simple conversations, you'll discover how the foundation you've built supports your ability to use Russian in real-life situations. It's a transformative phase that sets the stage for more advanced proficiency and deeper immersion in the language.

The Russian Learning Guide

Learn the Russian Cyrillic alphabet

Learn the Russian Cyrillic alphabet to be able to read Russian texts. That's what my workbook is for.

Learn Your First 720 Russian Words

The A1 level in Russian corresponds to approximately 700 words. You will learn these in this book, with the flashcards cut out and via the app.

Learn all the important rules of grammar

Understanding of the most important grammatical rules and sentence structures. I am currently working on a book about this.

Practicing conversations in everyday life

After the alphabet, vocabulary and grammar, you can now practise simple conversations and really make use of your new Russian language skills.

The unique learning method of this book

On the following pages, I will explain in detail how to use this book effectively. So read these pages really carefully. You can also learn on your own, but then you will probably take longer and be overwhelmed by the large amount of words to learn in this book. I have thought about this from the very beginning when creating this book and have worked out a precise learning method for it so that you can experience the best learning success. The less you deviate from it, the more I can guarantee your success. But in the end, it's entirely up to you.

Flashcards

The book is fundamentally based on flashcards. This may sound boring or old-fashioned to many, but scientifically (and in my experience) it is by far the most effective way of learning and remembering vocabulary.

Flashcards are small cards made of paper (from cut-out pages of this book in our case) that are printed on the front and back. On one side is the English word and on the other the Russian word. We have deliberately refrained from using a transcribed version of the Russian. Instead, only the word is written in Cyrillic on the cards. This is important because you should master the alphabet before you start learning vocabulary. So if you can't read the Russian Cyrillic alphabet yet, then put this book away for the next few days and learn the alphabet first. I explained the best way to do this in step 1 of my learning plan a few pages ago. Then you can pick up this book again. You don't have to know the alphabet perfectly, as learning the vocabulary will naturally give you an even better feel for it. But you do need to know it well enough to recognize most of the letters relatively quickly and, above all, to be able to distinguish the letters that at first glance look similar to our Latin letters from the Russian ones. In addition to the flashcards at the end of this book, we have also made all 720 words available via the Quizlet app. Most people actually learn more with the app than with the cards in my experience. I personally do the same. You can learn the app from anywhere, as you always have it with you on your smartphone. However, if you want to study with real paper, you can cut out the flashcards. You'll also find a QR code on page 211 that you can use to print out all 720 flashcards again. This was important to me so that you can simply print out new ones if you lose a card. At the same time, the paper of this book is of course not too thick, as it is a book. This doesn't bother me or most others, but I also know people who prefer to study with thicker paper for flashcards, which I can understand. You can also print out the cards on thicker paper and then study that way.

When you start learning, it makes sense to swap the front and back occasionally. This means once starting with the English first and another time starting with the Russian first. This helps your brain to form complex connections with the language more easily and to memorize the vocabulary. I will explain in a few pages how to start learning with flashcards and how many you should learn each day.

Vocabulary section

The book has a 180-page vocabulary section where you can look up all 720 words. There you will find the pronunciation and detailed explanations of the individual words that do not fit on a flashcard. You also have space to write the word a few times. This is not a writing book, but for those who have already worked through my first workbook, it makes sense to write each word 1-2 times yourself so that you don't get out of practice. If you want to write more, you can of course just take a normal sheet of paper and continue practicing your writing there.

Each noun entry also includes its grammatical gender—masculine, feminine, or neuter. This information is crucial for anyone learning Russian, as the gender of a noun determines how it declines in different grammatical cases and how its plural form is created. Understanding a noun's gender helps you apply the correct endings when using the word in context, ensuring accuracy when constructing sentences or working with adjectives and verbs.

For verbs, both their imperfective and perfective forms are included, as this pairing is essential to understanding how actions are expressed in Russian. Additionally, the book specifies the conjugation group of each verb, whether it follows the common patterns (-ать, -ить, etc.) or is irregular. Knowing how a verb conjugates will give you the tools to use it correctly across various subjects and tenses, setting the foundation for more advanced grammar later on.

There is also an example sentence for each word that shows the Russian word in practice. As Russian words have different word forms and you are primarily learning the dictionary form in this book, it is possible that the words in the example sentences have taken on a different form. However, the words are always marked in bold so that you can recognize which word in the sentence is the respective vocabulary word.

This combination of detailed explanations, gender and aspect information, and example sentences ensures that you not only learn the words themselves but also understand how they function within the broader context of the Russian language.

On the next page you will now find my detailed learning strategy for the flashcards and access to the Quizlet app

The Importance of Stress in Russian

In Russian, stress—the emphasis on a specific syllable in a word—plays a crucial role in pronunciation and meaning. As in English, stress in Russian can vary greatly and is not marked in the written language. This means that the same word with different stresses can have completely different meanings or grammatical forms. For example, замок (zámok) means "castle," while замок (zamók) means "lock."

To help you navigate this, each Russian word in this book includes a transcription with a stress mark (´) over the vowel that should be emphasized. This ensures that you pronounce the word correctly and avoid misunderstandings.

Mastering stress is essential for clear communication in Russian. Incorrect stress can make words difficult for native speakers to understand and may change the meaning of what you're trying to say. By paying attention to the marked stress in this book, you'll develop better pronunciation and a more natural flow when speaking Russian.

The learning method:

The basics

The basic idea behind this learning strategy is consistency. Means learning every day. How much is up to you. Ideally 8, 16 or 24 new words every day.
We make a deck every 48 cards. No more cards are removed from this deck and no more new cards are added. It is fixed. If you learn 8 new words a day, you will have a new deck every six days. With 16 you need three days and with 24 only two days.

Learning with decks (15 x 48 cards)

Until you have your first deck, you will learn new words every day and repeat all the old ones. As soon as you have the first deck, you learn it daily as a unit and in addition you continue to take new cards daily and make the next deck with them. As soon as you have two decks, you ideally learn both of them every day + the new cards that you take every day and make a third deck with them. The goal is always to learn at least the last 2 decks + the new deck you are building. In addition, you should learn each of the old decks 1-2 times a week for repetition. The aim is to have 15 decks of 48 flashcards at the end of this book.

Learn daily

Learning a deck means going through it at least 2 times, better 3 times. You should go through new cards 4-5 times a day. With the Quizlet app, you can also repeat only the wrong ones and thus save some time.
I recommend shuffling the decks and starting from a different side every few days. So start a few days with Russian first and then with English first. Switching it up again and again will challenge you, but will improve your overall learning speed.

Recommendation depending on personal time

If you have less than 15 minutes a day, I recommend that you learn 8 new words a day and repeat 1 deck a day and in addition to the new deck you are building. More is difficult with so little time. With 15-30 minutes, I recommend you learn 16-24 new cards per day and the last two decks daily, in addition to the new deck you are building. With 30+ minutes a day, you can definitely learn 24 new cards a day and repeat 3+ decks a day and learn the new deck you are building

Quizlet access

In addition to this book, I have also made all 720 flashcards available to you free of charge via the Quizlet learning platform. So if you prefer to learn via smartphone app, instead of having to cut out all the flashcards, you can also learn digitally! Find out how to get access here:

This is how you get access:

1. Scan the QR code

Below you will find a QR code or a link. Scan the code or type in the link. Then enter your e-mail address so that your Quizlet access can be sent to you. If you have already installed the Quizlet app, you will be forwarded directly. If you don't have an account yet, you will find an explanation in the confirmation email of exactly how you need to proceed to get free access to the vocabulary and the Quizlet app:

www.self-taught-languages.com/your-first-720-words-in-russian/

2. Flashcard sets as digital decks

The Quizlet Flashcard sets are structured in exactly the same way as the 15 decks. The disadvantage of Quizlet is that you can only ever learn the complete decks and not start with 8 as I recommend and add 8 new ones every day. But if that doesn't bother you, you can learn directly in complete decks. A few pages further on in the Q&A I also have a trick that avoids this problem

3. Practise correctly

In addition to the normal function of flashcards, Quizlet offers many other exercises and even games to add variety to your learning process. Quizlet can also read the words to you. In Russian, the pronunciation of words is very important and can change the meaning of entire words. I therefore recommend having Quizlet read each word to you again and again. In the bonus module (at the bottom) you can also focus on learning numbers, days of the week, seasons and times.

Grammatical basics

This is not a grammar book. It's a vocabulary book that will help you build an A1 vocabulary in record time. However, in order to be able to interpret some vocabulary correctly, at least a basic understanding of grammar is important.

If you have seen my plan, then you will have seen that I recommend grammar only after vocabulary. This is because vocabulary provides real, tangible moments of success more quickly and keeps you motivated for longer. So if you already have a basic understanding of Russian grammar, you probably won't find anything new here. The following pages are aimed at absolute beginners so that they have enough knowledge to learn the vocabulary appropriately.

Since you should mainly focus on vocabulary with this book and grammar rules should not distract you, I have kept this theory section as short as possible. I am currently working on a book that focuses exclusively on Russian grammar and sentence structure. It will be the 3rd book in my Russian textbook series and therefore covers the 3rd step of my learning plan. If you would like to be informed as soon as it is published, you can sign up via the following link or just scan the QR code, and you will be the first to receive an e-mail notification:

www.self-taught-languages.com/new-russian-textbook/

Verbs

Russian verbs are categorized into two main conjugation groups based on their infinitive endings: -ать, -ить, -еть, etc. Each group follows predictable patterns for conjugation, making it easier to identify how a verb changes depending on the subject. Throughout this book, every verb is labeled with its conjugation group, so that you can look up the conjugation here.

Nouns

Russian nouns change their endings depending on their grammatical case, which determines their role in a sentence (subject, object, possession, etc.). These changes, called declensions, are influenced by the noun's gender: masculine, feminine, or neuter. While this book doesn't explain every case in detail, it does include the gender of each noun to help you recognize the patterns of declension as you learn.

Adjectives

Adjectives in Russian must adapt in gender, number and case to the nouns they describe. In their simplest form, they have special endings based on the gender of the noun. The endings also change depending on the case of the noun (e.g. in the genitive or accusative case). We don't have anything like this in English. Beautiful woman, beautiful man and beautiful house all have the same "beautiful" in front of them. In Russian, the ending of beautiful would change each time, depending on gender and case.

The three main verb groups

In Russian, verbs change their endings depending on the subject of the sentence (I, you, he, she, it, we, you (plural/formal), they). This process is called conjugation. Russian verbs belong to different conjugation groups, each with its own set of endings in the present tense. Below is a comprehensive table for the three main verb groups, showing the full conjugation and their respective endings side by side for clarity.

1. Verbs ending in -ать (e.g., читать – to read)

Most verbs in this group belong to the 1st conjugation:

Person	Conjugated Form	Ending
Я (I)	Я читаю (I read)	-ю
Ты (You)	Ты читаешь (You read)	-ешь
Он/она/оно (He/She/It)	Он читает (He reads)	-ет
Мы (We)	Мы читаем (We read)	-ем
Вы (You - plural/formal)	Вы читаете (You read)	-ете
Они (They)	Они читают (They read)	-ют

2. Verbs ending in -ить (e.g., говорить – to speak)

Most verbs in this group belong to the 2nd conjugation.

Person	Conjugated Form	Ending
Я (I)	Я говорю (I speak)	-ю
Ты (You)	Ты говоришь (You speak)	-ишь
Он/она/оно (He/She/It)	Он говорит (He speaks)	-ит
Мы (We)	Мы говорим (We speak)	-им
Вы (You - plural/formal)	Вы говорите (You speak)	-ите
Они (They)	Они говорят (They speak)	-ят

3. Verbs ending in -еть (e.g., смотреть – to watch)

Most -еть verbs follow the 2nd conjugation, though some exceptions exist.

Person	Conjugated Form	Ending
Я (I)	Я смотрю (I watch)	-ю
Ты (You)	Ты смотришь (You watch)	-ишь
Он/она/оно (He/She/It)	Он смотрит (He watches)	-ит
Мы (We)	Мы смотрим (We watch)	-им
Вы (You - plural/formal)	Вы смотрите (You watch)	-ите
Они (They)	Они смотрят (They watch)	-ят

Irregular verbs

Irregular verbs in Russian are verbs that do not follow the standard conjugation patterns of the main verb groups. While most Russian verbs belong to these regular conjugation patterns, irregular verbs have unique changes in their stems or endings that make them exceptions to the rules.

These verbs often reflect some of the most common and essential actions or states in the language, such as "to be," "to go," "to eat," or "to want." Because they are frequently used in everyday speech, learning their unique conjugations is critical for effective communication. Unlike regular verbs, which have predictable endings based on their conjugation group, irregular verbs may change their stems, vowels, or endings in ways that need to be memorized individually.

In this book, all irregular verbs are marked as such. If you have registered on Quizlet, you will also receive additional learning material from me by e-mail. There you will also find a table of all A1 irregular verbs, with all their conjugations, which you can use to learn them. These are the most important irregular verbs in their dictionary form:

- быть – to be
- идти – to go (one direction, by foot)
- ходить – to go (multidirectional, by foot)
- есть – to eat
- пить – to drink
- дать – to give
- мочь – to be able to / can
- хотеть – to want
- знать – to know

Aspects of Verbs

In Russian, verbs are categorized into two aspects: perfective and imperfective, which describe how an action is perceived in terms of completion. This distinction is unique to Russian and is essential for expressing nuances of time and intention.

The imperfective aspect is used to describe actions that are incomplete, ongoing, habitual, or repeated. It focuses on the process of the action rather than the result. For example, the verb писать (to write) in the imperfective aspect implies the act of writing without specifying whether it has been completed. Imperfective verbs are often used in the present tense to describe ongoing actions and in the past tense to describe actions that were in progress or repeated.

In contrast, the perfective aspect is used to describe actions that are viewed as complete or as having a definite result. For example, the verb написать (to write, perfective) implies that the writing has been finished. Perfective verbs do not exist in the present tense; instead, they refer to actions that will be completed in the future or were completed in the past.

Each verb in Russian typically comes in a pair, with one form being imperfective and the other perfective. These pairs allow speakers to choose how they want to present the action: as a process or as a completed event. For example:

- Imperfective: читать (to read, focusing on the process or habit).
- Perfective: прочитать (to read, focusing on the completion of the act).

In the vocabulary section of this book, both forms of a verb are always listed together. I have also decided to write both aspects on the Russian side of the flashcards. The imperfective is at the top of the flashcards for verbs and the perfective is at the bottom. This way, you not only learn the action itself, but also how to use it in both aspects. By understanding these pairs, you will develop a deeper understanding of how to express time and intention in Russian and conjugate sentences that accurately convey the nuances of your thoughts.

Introduction to Nouns

In Russian, nouns play a central role in sentences and are far more dynamic than in English. They are categorized by gender, change form based on grammatical case, and are further distinguished as animate or inanimate, all of which influence their endings and how they interact with other words.

Every Russian noun belongs to one of three genders: masculine, feminine, or neuter. The gender of a noun determines how it behaves in sentences and how it interacts with adjectives, verbs, and other parts of speech. For example, masculine nouns typically end in a consonant or -й, feminine nouns often end in -а or -я, and neuter nouns usually end in -о, -е, or occasionally -мя. These gendered endings are critical, as they influence the noun's declension patterns when used in different grammatical cases.

Grammatical cases

Nouns also change their endings based on grammatical case, which reflects their role in a sentence. Russian has six cases:

- **Nominative**, which identifies the subject of the sentence;
- **Genitive**, which expresses possession, absence, or quantity;
- **Dative**, which indicates the indirect object;
- **Accusative**, which marks the direct object;
- **Instrumental**, which shows the means by which an action is performed;
- **Prepositional**, which is used with certain prepositions to indicate location, topic, or context

Each case has its own set of endings, which vary depending on the noun's gender and whether it is singular or plural. These endings are essential for understanding and constructing correct sentences.

Russian nouns are further divided into animate and inanimate categories. This distinction is particularly important in the accusative case. Inanimate nouns use the same form in the accusative case as in the nominative case, while animate nouns take the form of the genitive case. For example, я вижу стол (I see the table) uses the nominative form for the inanimate noun стол, whereas я вижу мужчину (I see the man) uses the genitive form мужчину for the animate noun мужчина. This rule applies to both singular and plural forms.

Understanding these key aspects—gender, cases, and the distinction between animate and inanimate nouns—is vital for using Russian nouns correctly. These grammatical features determine how nouns interact with other words in sentences, and mastering them is an important step in building your proficiency in Russian.

The three genders of nouns

These are the most common endings of the three genders:

Gender	Common Endings	Examples
Masculine	-й, -ь, consonant	стол (table) чай (tea) конь (horse)
Feminine	-а, -я, -ь	книга (book) земля (earth) дверь (door)
Neuter	-о, -е, -мя	окно (window) море (sea) время (time)

Plural Formation

Plural endings depend on the gender of the noun:

Gender	Singular Ending	Plural Ending	Examples
Masculine	-й, -ь, consonant	-и / -ы	музей музеи (museum museums) стол столы (table tables)
Feminine	-а, -я, -ь	-и / -ы	книга книги (book books) земля земли (earth earths)
Neuter	-о, -е, -мя	-а / -я	окно окна (window windows) море моря (sea seas)

Cases and Endings (Singular)

The six cases in Russian dictate how noun endings change depending on their grammatical function. Here are the endings for each gender in singular:

Case	Masculine	Feminine	Neuter
Nominative	-й, -ь, consonant	-а, -я, -ь	-о, -е
Genitive	-а / -я	-ы / -и	-а / -я
Dative	-у / -ю	-е	-у / -ю
Accusative	(like Nom/Gen)*	(like Nom/Gen)*	-о, -е
Instrumental	-ом / -ем	-ой / -ей	-ом / -ем
Prepositional	-е	-е	-е

*In the accusative case, inanimate nouns use the same form as in the nominative case, while animate nouns take the form of the genitive case.

23

Cases and Endings (Plural)

The endings of nouns in the plural are almost always the same, regardless of gender and case. However, as there are 1-2 exceptions, you can find everything listed here in a table:

Case	Masculine	Feminine	Neuter
Nominative	-ы / -и	-ы / -и	-а / -я
Genitive	-ов / -ев / -ей	- / -ей	- / -ей
Dative	-ам	-ам	-ам
Accusative	(like Nom/Gen)**	(like Nom/Gen)**	-а / -я
Instrumental	-ами	-ами	-ами
Prepositional	-ах	-ах	-ах

*In the accusative case, inanimate nouns use the same form as in the nominative case, while animate nouns take the form of the genitive case.

Introduction to Adjectives

Adjectives in Russian agree with the gender, number, and case of the noun they describe. This means the ending of an adjective changes to match the grammatical form of the noun. Although this may seem complex at first, Russian adjectives follow predictable patterns, which makes them relatively easy to learn with practice.

Case	Masculine	Feminine	Neuter	Plural
Nominative	-ый / -ий	-ая	-ое	-ые / -ие
Genitive	-ого	-ой	-ого	-ых
Dative	-ому	-ой	-ому	-ым
Accusative	(like Nom/Gen)*	(like Nom/Gen)*	-ое	(like Nom/Gen)*
Instrumental	-ым	-ой	-ым	-ыми
Prepositional	-ом	-ой	-ом	-ых

Q&A

Why 48 cards per deck?

48 is a convenient number to practice several times a day. Also, with 720 vocabulary words, we have to categorize the cards somehow so that you don't just learn any cards. The 15 decks allow you to see each one as a single unit. When you get good at a deck, you can put it aside and practice it less and less often. If we didn't have decks, you would always be learning random vocabulary and the whole strategy would have no order or structure at all.

How do I learn best with Quizlet?

Quizlet has the disadvantage that you cannot add 8, 16 or 24 individual cards per day as I would recommend. This is because only the full blocks are available in Quizlet. However, you can get around this with a trick: If you set Quizlet to not shuffle the deck, it will always be in the same order. If you then reopen the flashcard function every day, you always start with the same words. So you can do 8 on the first day, 16 on the second, 24 on the third, 32 on the fourth, and so on until you have gone through the whole deck. Then you can shuffle the deck for the first time and practice it as a whole. With the next deck, simply proceed step by step in the same way as you did here.

When you've finished them, click on the back arrow at the bottom left several times to return to the beginning so that you can go through these 8 again. You can keep going until you have mastered all 8.

This will go quickly, especially at the beginning, and if you have more than 15 minutes a day to learn, I recommend learning 16 a day. That's a lot and a bit challenging, but this challenge also makes learning exciting and motivates you to keep at it.

Do you recommend learning with Quizlet or with cards?

Both have advantages and disadvantages, it depends more on what suits you more as a person. If you are easily distracted by your cell phone, it may make more sense to study with real cards so that you are not distracted by notifications on your cell phone.

At the same time, Quizlet has many technical advantages. In addition to the flashcard function, it has many other functions and games that can make learning more varied. It also saves your progress, and you can track how well you have learned all the vocabulary so far. It can also send you reminders so that you study every day.

But what I would definitely recommend Quizlet for is to listen to all the words. Quizlet can read every word to you. Since stress is very important in Russian and can change the meaning of whole words, this is essential to learn a correct pronunciation.

I personally prefer to practice with Quizlet, which is why it was important to me to include the app in this book for free. I travel a lot and like to learn on the go. This also works with individual flashcard decks, but not with all 720 cards. That's why I really like the app.

What if I have problems with Quizlet?

If you have problems logging in to the Quizlet app or getting access to the course, you are welcome to send me an e-mail to russian@self-taught-languages.com and I will try to solve the problem.

What if I don't yet know the Russian Cyrillic alphabet?

I would recommend that you first learn the alphabet before you start intensive vocabulary training. Although you always have a transcribed version in the vocabulary section of this book, this is primarily intended to teach you the correct pronunciation.
On the flashcards, as in Quizlet, you only have the Russian word. There is enough space on the flashcards to write the transcription under the Russian word, but I wouldn't recommend that.
You can also have the words read out to you on Quizlet. In my opinion, this is the best learning method as it allows you to learn the pronunciation correctly from the start.
You can learn the alphabet with online materials, or you can make your own flashcards using the tables on the first pages of this book. If you want to perfect the alphabet straight away and also learn to write it, I recommend my first textbook.

Would you recommend learning together?

If you have the option, I would always recommend having someone to hold you accountable. This could be friends, family or your partner. Ideally, you'll have someone you can even study with. Then you can check up on each other and eventually speak together. Having someone to talk to is a huge advantage when you're learning a new language.

What is the best way to learn with friends?

It's best to have a fixed appointment once a week to discuss how the last week went. It doesn't have to be longer than 10 minutes if you're both very busy. It's more about having someone to check up on you. For example, you could agree to practise for 20 minutes every day and then meet briefly or talk on the phone every Friday. Basically, it doesn't matter whether you know your study partner personally or whether you met them via a Facebook group or the internet in general, for example. There are even special Facebook groups for Russian learning partners (and for other languages too).

Thanks for reading the introduction - and now good luck and have fun practicing!

Vocabulary section

The following 180 pages consist of the vocabulary section of this book. This is followed by the flashcards to cut out.

The vocabulary section serves as a reference work. While you are practicing with the flashcards, you can always refer back to the vocabulary section and find context for the respective word. For example, each word also has an example sentence so that you can see it in context. It makes sense to always look at new vocabulary here in the vocabulary section so that you really know exactly what it means and how it is used.

The Russian words are always in their basic form / dictionary form. Depending on gender and case, these words can change, so it may be that the word in the example sentences is spelled slightly differently than the dictionary form. You learned why the form changes and how in the previous chapter. However, this may not matter to you at the beginning, as the focus is foremost on learning the vocabulary. Applying cases, gender and tenses to the vocabulary is the third step in my learning plan and therefore not the aim of this book. .

Next to the Russian words you will always find the pronunciation with our letters and a ' above the letter (for example: á) that is stressed in the Russian word. Stress is very important, but is not normally obvious to us from the writing, so we mark it for you to practice. However, this marking is missing on the flashcards, which is why the vocabulary section is important for learning the pronunciation correctly.

I also recommend that you have each vocabulary word recited several times on Quizlet. Although it helps to have the pronunciation marked in the vocabulary section, it is something completely different when you actually hear the words in the Quizlet App.

автобус | ávtobus

Part of speech: noun

Gender: masculine

Bus, as in "I wait for the **bus** every morning" (Я жду **автобус** каждое утро.).
It is a noun and is often used to describe a vehicle used for public transport.

автобус автобус

автобус автобус

bus

автобусная остановка | ávtobusnaya ostanóvka

Part of speech: noun phrase

Gender: feminine

Bus stop, as in "I waited at the **bus stop**" (Я ждал на **автобусной остановке**.). It is a noun phrase and is used to describe a designated place where buses pick up or drop off passengers.

автобусная остановка

bus stop

автовокзал | ávtovokzal

Part of speech: noun

Gender: masculine

Bus station, as in "The **bus station** is located in the city center" (**Автовокзал** находится в центре города.). It is a noun and is used to describe a terminal for long-distance buses.

автовокзал

bus station

автоспорт | ávtosport

Part of speech: noun

Gender: masculine

Motorsport, as in "**Motorsport** is popular all over the world" (**Автоспорт** популярен по всему миру.). It is a noun and is used to describe sports involving racing or competitive driving.

автоспорт

motorsport

адвокат | advokát

Part of speech: noun

Gender: masculine

Lawyer, as in "The **lawyer** helped with the case" (**Адвокат** помог с делом.).
It is a noun and is used to describe a person who practices law and represents clients.

адвокат

lawyer

айти-специалист | aití-spetsialíst

Part of speech: noun

Gender: masculine

IT specialist, as in "The **IT specialist** fixed the computer" (**Айти-специалист**
починил компьютер.). It is a noun and is used to describe a person who
works in information technology and manages computer systems or networks.

айти – специалист

IT specialist

апельсин | apelsín

Part of speech: noun

Gender: masculine

Orange, as in "I eat an **orange** every day" (Я ем **апельсин** каждый день.).
It is a noun and is used to describe a type of citrus fruit.

апельсин

orange

аптека | aptéka

Part of speech: noun

Gender: feminine

Pharmacy, as in "I bought medicine at the **pharmacy**" (Я купил лекарство в **аптеке**.).
It is a noun and is used to describe a place where medications and health products are sold.

аптека

pharmacy

арендованный автомобиль | arendóvannyy avtomobíl'

Part of speech: noun phrase

Gender: masculine

Rented car, as in "He drove a **rented car** on vacation" (Он ездил на **арендованном автомобиле** в отпуске.). It is a noun phrase and is used to describe a vehicle that has been rented temporarily for personal use

арендованный автомобиль

rented car

аэропорт | aeroport

Part of speech: noun

Gender: masculine

Airport, as in "The **airport** is busy today" (**Аэропорт** сегодня многолюден.).
It is a noun and is used to refer to a place where aircraft take off and land.

аэропорт

airport

багаж | bagázh

Part of speech: noun

Gender: masculine

Luggage, as in "I need to check my **luggage** at the airport" (Мне нужно сдать **багаж** в аэропорту.).
It is a noun and is used to refer to the bags and suitcases that travelers take with them.

багаж

luggage

банан | banán

Part of speech: noun

Gender: masculine

Banana, as in "I like to eat a **banana** for breakfast" (Мне нравится есть **банан** на завтрак.).
It is a noun and is used to refer to a long, curved fruit with a yellow skin and soft, sweet flesh inside.

банан

banana

банк | bánk

Part of speech: noun

Gender: masculine

Bank, as in "I need to go to the **bank** to withdraw some money" (Мне нужно пойти в **банк**, чтобы снять деньги.). It is a noun and is used to refer to a financial institution that accepts deposits and provides loans.

банк

bank

банкомат | bankomát

Part of speech: noun

Gender: masculine

ATM, as in "I need to find an **ATM** to withdraw cash" (Мне нужно найти **банкомат**, чтобы снять наличные.). It is a noun and is used to refer to a machine that allows people to access their bank accounts to withdraw cash, deposit money, or check their balance.

банкомат

ATM

бар | bár

Part of speech: noun

Gender: masculine

Bar, as in "We went to a **bar** to have some drinks" (Мы пошли в **бар**, чтобы выпить.). It is a noun and is used to refer to an establishment that serves alcoholic beverages and often food.

бар

bar

баскетбол | basketból

Part of speech: noun

Gender: masculine

Basketball, as in "I enjoy playing **basketball** with my friends" (Мне нравится играть в **баскетбол** с друзьями.). It is a noun and is used to refer to a team sport in which two teams try to score points by throwing a ball through the opponent's hoop.

баскетбол

basketball

бег | bég

Part of speech: noun

Gender: masculine

Running, as in "**Running** is a great way to stay fit" (**Бег** — отличный способ поддерживать форму.). It is a noun and is used to describe the act of moving swiftly on foot.

бег

running

бедный | bédnyy

Part of speech: adjective

Poor, as in "The **poor** man needs help" (**Бедный** человек нуждается в помощи.). It is an adjective and is often used to describe someone lacking sufficient money or resources.

бедный

poor

бедро | bédro

Part of speech: noun

Gender: neuter

Hip, as in "He injured his **hip** while playing sports" (Он повредил **бедро**, играя в спорт.). It is a noun and is used to describe the joint between the thigh and the pelvis.

бедро

hip

бежать | bezhát́ (Imperfective)

Part of speech: verb
Verb group: irregular

Perfective: побежать | pobezhát'

Run, as in "I need to **run** to catch the bus" (Мне нужно **бежать**, чтобы успеть на автобус.). It is a verb and is used to describe moving quickly on foot.

бежать

to run

безопасность | bezopásnost'

Part of speech: noun

Gender: feminine

Security, as in "Data **security** is very important" (**Безопасность** данных очень важна.).
It is a noun and is often used to describe the state of being safe from physical or digital threats.

безопасность

security, safety

безопасный | bezopásnyy

Part of speech: adjective

Safe, as in "This area is considered **safe**" (Этот район считается **безопасным.**).
It is an adjective and is used to describe something free from danger or risk.

безопасный

safe

билет | bilét

Part of speech: noun

Gender: masculine

Ticket, as in "I bought a **ticket** to the concert" (Я купил **билет** на концерт.).
It is a noun and is used to describe a pass or document that grants entry or access to an event or transportation.

билет

ticket

благодарить | blagodarít' (Imperfective)

Part of speech: verb
Verb group: -ить

Perfective: поблагодарить | poblagodarít'

Thank, as in "I **thank** you for your help" (Я **благодарю** тебя за помощь.).
It is a verb and is used to express gratitude towards someone.

благодарить

to thank

богатый | bogátyy

Part of speech: adjective

Rich, as in "He is a **rich** man" (Он **богатый** человек.). It is an adjective and is used to describe someone who has a lot of wealth or resources.

богатый

rich

бодрый | bódryy

Part of speech: adjective

Awake, as in "After a good night's sleep, I feel cheerful and **awake**" (После хорошего сна я чувствую себя **бодрым**.). It is an adjective and is used to describe someone who is energetic, alert, and in good spirits.

бодрый

awake

бокс | bóks

Gender: masculine

Part of speech: noun

Boxing, as in "He trains in **boxing** every day" (Он тренируется в **боксе** каждый день.). It is a noun and is used to describe the sport of fighting with gloves in a boxing ring.

бокс

boxing

больница | bol'nítsa

Gender: feminine

Part of speech: noun

Hospital, as in "She was taken to the **hospital** for treatment" (Её увезли в **больницу** для лечения.). It is a noun and is used to describe a facility where patients receive medical care and treatment.

больница

hospital

больничный лист | bol'níchny list

Part of speech: noun

Gender: masculine

Sick leave, as in "He took **sick leave** after his surgery" (Он взял **больничный лист** после операции.).
It is a noun and is used to refer to both the document certifying illness and the time off work that one takes due to health issues.

больничный лист

sick leave

больной | bol'nóy

Part of speech: adjective

Sick, as in "The **sick** person needs to see a doctor" (**Больной** человек нуждается в враче.).
It is used as an adjective to describe someone who is unwell, and as a noun, it refers to a patient in a medical context.

больной

sick

большой | bol'shóy

Part of speech: adjective

Big, as in "They have a **big** house" (У них **большой** дом.). It is an adjective and is used to describe something of considerable size or extent.

большой

big

большой палец | bol'shóy pálets

Part of speech: noun

Gender: masculine

Thumb, as in "He injured his **thumb** while playing" (Он повредил **большой палец** во время игры.).
It is a noun and is used to refer to the short, thick digit on the hand, which is opposable to the other fingers.

большой палец

thumb

борода | borodá

Part of speech: noun

Gender: feminine

Beard, as in "He decided to grow a **beard**" (Он решил отрастить **бороду**.). It is a noun and is used to describe the hair that grows on the chin and cheeks of a man's face.

борода

beard

борьба | bor'bá

Part of speech: noun

Gender: feminine

Wrestling, as in "He trains in **wrestling** every week" (Он тренируется в **борьбе** каждую неделю.). It is a noun and is used to describe both a physical or metaphorical fight against opposition and the sport of wrestling itself.

борьба

wrestling

брат | brát

Part of speech: noun

Gender: masculine

Brother, as in "My **brother** is coming to visit" (Мой **брат** приезжает в гости.). It is a noun and is used to refer to a male sibling.

брат

brother

брать | brát' (Imperfective)

Part of speech: verb
Verb group: irregular

Perfective: взять | vzyát'

To take, as in "I want **to take** this book" (Я хочу **взять** эту книгу.). It is a verb and is often used to describe the action of picking up or receiving something.

брать

to take

будний день | búdniy dyén'

Part of speech: noun

Gender: masculine

Weekday, as in "I work every **weekday**" (Я работаю каждый **будний день**.).
It is a noun and is used to refer to the days of the week when most people work,
typically Monday through Friday.

будний день

weekday

бурно | búrno

Part of speech: adverb

Stormy, as in "The weather was **stormy** yesterday" (Погода была **бурной**
вчера.). It is an adverb and is often used to describe conditions that are
turbulent or intense.

бурно

stormy, violently

бухгалтер | buhgal'tér

Part of speech: noun

Gender: masculine

Accountant, as in "The **accountant** prepares the financial statements" (**Бухгалтер** составляет
финансовые отчёты.). It is a noun and is used to refer to a person responsible for financial
record-keeping and reporting in an organization.

бухгалтер

accountant

быстро | bístro

Part of speech: adverb

Quickly, as in "She runs **quickly** to catch the bus" (Она **быстро** бегает, чтобы успеть на автобус.).
It is an adverb and is used to describe an action that occurs at a high speed or in a short amount of
time.

быстро

quickly, fast

быстрый | býstryy

Part of speech: adjective

Fast, as in "He has a **fast** car" (У него **быстрая** машина.). It is an adjective and is often used to describe something that moves or happens at high speed.

быстрый

fast, quick

быть | byt' (Imperfective)

Part of speech: verb
Verb group: irregular

Perfective: none

To be, as in "I want **to be** happy" (Я хочу **быть** счастливым.). It is a verb and is commonly used as a basic verb indicating existence, state, or condition.

быть

to be

в основном | v osnovnóm

Part of speech: adverb

Mainly, as in "He **mainly** studies in the evening" (Он **в основном** учится вечером.). It is an adverb and is often used to describe the primary or most frequent part of an action or situation.

в основном

mainly, mostly

в прошлом году | v próshlom godú

Part of speech: adverbial phrase

Last year, as in "We traveled to Europe **last year**" (Мы путешествовали в Европу **в прошлом году**.). It is an adverbial phrase and is used to refer to the year preceding the current one.

в прошлом году

last year

в следующем году | v sléduyushchem godú

Next year, as in "We will go on vacation **next year**" (Мы поедем в отпуск **в следующем году**.).
It is an adverbial phrase and is used to refer to the year following the current one.

в следующем году

next year

в то время как | v to vrémya kak

While, as in "She likes coffee, **while** he prefers tea" (Она любит кофе, **в то время как** он предпочитает чай.). It is a conjunction and is often used to contrast two actions or situations happening at the same time.

в то время как

while

важный| vázhnyy

Important, as in "This is an **important** decision" (Это **важное** решение.).
It is an adjective and is often used to describe something of great significance or value.

важный

important

вдруг | vdruk

Suddenly, as in "**Suddenly**, he appeared at the door" (**Вдруг** он появился у двери.).
It is an adverb and is often used to describe an unexpected event or change that happens unexpectedly.

вдруг

suddenly

везде | vezdée

Part of speech: adverb

Everywhere, as in "I looked **everywhere** for my keys" (Я искал свои ключи **везде**.).
It is an adverb and is often used to indicate that something is present in all places or locations.

везде

everywhere

век | vek

Part of speech: noun

Gender: masculine

Century, as in "We are living in the 21st **century**" (Мы живём в 21 **веке**.).
It is a noun and is often used to describe a period of one hundred years.

век

century

велосипед | velosipéd

Part of speech: noun

Gender: masculine

Bicycle, as in "He bought a new **bicycle**" (Он купил новый **велосипед**.). It is a noun and is used to describe a two-wheeled vehicle powered by pedals, often used for transportation, sports, or leisure.

велосипед

bicycle

вероятно | veroyátno

Part of speech: adverb

Probably, as in "She will **probably** come to the party" (Она, **вероятно**, придёт на вечеринку.).
It is an adverb and is often used to indicate a likelihood or assumption about something.

вероятно

probably

верховая езда | verkhováya ezdá

Part of speech: noun phrase

Gender: feminine

Horse riding, as in "She enjoys **horse riding** on weekends" (Она любит **верховую езду** по выходным.). It is a noun phrase and is often used to refer to the activity or sport of riding horses.

верховая езда

horse riding

весенний день | vesénniy den'

Part of speech: noun phrase

Gender: masculine

Spring day, as in "A warm **spring day** is perfect for a walk" (Тёплый **весенний день** идеально подходит для прогулки.). It is a noun phrase and is often used to describe a day during the spring season.

весенний день

spring day

весна | vesná

Part of speech: noun

Gender: feminine

Spring, as in "**Spring** brings blooming flowers" (**Весна** приносит цветущие цветы.). It is a noun and is often used to refer to the season following winter and preceding summer.

весна

spring

ветер | véter

Part of speech: noun

Gender: masculine

Wind, as in "The **wind** is strong today" (Сегодня сильный **ветер**.). It is a noun and is often used to describe moving air, especially in the context of weather.

ветер

wind

ветрено | vétreno

Part of speech: adverb

Windy, as in "It's very **windy** outside" (На улице очень **ветрено**.).
It is an adverb and is often used to describe weather conditions with a lot of wind.

ветрено

windy

вечер | vécher

Part of speech: noun

Gender: masculine

Evening, as in "We went for a walk in the **evening**" (Мы пошли на прогулку **вечером**.).
It is a noun and is often used to refer to the time of day between afternoon and night.

вечер

evening

видеть | vídet' (Imperfective)

Part of speech: verb
Verb group: -еть

Perfective: увидеть | uvídet'

To see, as in "I can **see** the mountains from here" (Я могу **видеть** горы отсюда.). It is a
verb and is often used to describe the ability or act of perceiving something with the eyes.

видеть

to see

виза | víza

Part of speech: noun

Gender: feminine

Visa, as in "I need a **visa** to travel to that country" (Мне нужна **виза**, чтобы поехать в эту страну.).
It is a noun and is often used to refer to a document allowing entry into a foreign country.

виза

visa

вилка | vílka

Part of speech: noun

Gender: feminine

Fork, as in "Please pass me the **fork**" (Пожалуйста, передай мне **вилку**.).
It is a noun and is often used to refer to a utensil used for eating.

вилка

fork

вино | vinó

Part of speech: noun

Gender: neuter

Wine, as in "We enjoyed a glass of **wine** with dinner" (Мы наслаждались бокалом **вина** за ужином.).
It is a noun and is often used to refer to an alcoholic beverage made from fermented grapes.

вино

wine

влажно | bezháť

Part of speech: adverb

Humid, as in "It feels **humid** outside today" (Сегодня на улице **влажно**.). It is an adverb
and is often used to describe the weather condition with a high level of moisture in the air.

влажно

humid

вместе | vméste

Part of speech: adverb

Together, as in "We worked **together** on the project" (Мы работали **вместе** над проектом.).
It is an adverb and is often used to describe doing something jointly or in cooperation with others.

вместе

together

внизу | vnizú

Part of speech: adverb

Below, as in "The instructions are written **below** the diagram" (Инструкции написаны **внизу** под диаграммой.). It describes something located at a lower position on the same page or surface.

внизу

below

внутри | vnutrí

Part of speech: adverb

Inside, as in "The keys are **inside** the drawer" (Ключи находятся **внутри** ящика.).
It is an adverb used to describe something located within an enclosed space.

внутри

inside

вода | vodá

Gender: feminine

Part of speech: noun

Water, as in "Please pour me a glass of **water**" (Пожалуйста, налей мне стакан **воды**.).
It is a noun and refers to the clear, colorless liquid that is essential for life.

вода

water

водитель | vodítel'

Gender: masculine

Part of speech: noun

Driver, as in "The **driver** stopped the bus at the station" (**Водитель** остановил автобус на станции.). It refers to a person who operates a vehicle.

водитель

driver

вокзал | vokzál

Part of speech: noun

Gender: masculine

Train station, as in "We will meet at the **train station**" (Мы встретимся на **вокзале**.).
It refers to a facility where trains load or unload passengers or goods.

вокзал

train station

волейбол | volejból

Part of speech: noun

Gender: masculine

Volleyball, as in "She plays **volleyball** every weekend" (Она играет в **волейбол** каждые выходные.). It refers to the sport where two teams hit a ball over a net using their hands.

волейбол

volleyball

волос | vólos

Part of speech: noun

Gender: masculine

Hair, as in "A single **hair** fell on the table" (Один **волос** упал на стол.).
It refers to a single strand of hair.

волос

hair

восемнадцать | vosemnádtsat'

Part of speech: numeral

Eighteen, as in "She is **eighteen** years old" (Ей **восемнадцать** лет.).
It is used to denote the number 18. You can practice all the numbers together in the bonus module on Quizlet.

восемнадцать

eighteen

восемь | vósem'

Part of speech: numeral

Eight, as in "The clock struck **eight**" (Часы пробили **восемь**.).
It is used to denote the number 8.

восемь

eight

восемьдесят | vósem'desyat

Part of speech: numeral

Eighty, as in "The book has **eighty** pages" (В книге **восемьдесят** страниц.).
It is used to denote the number 80.

восемьдесят

eighty

восемьсот | vósem'sot

Part of speech: numeral

Eight hundred, as in "The library has **eight hundred** books" (В библиотеке **восемьсот** книг.). It is used to denote the number 800.

восемьсот

eight hundred

воскресенье | voskresén'ye

Part of speech: noun

Gender: neuter

Sunday, as in "We will meet on **Sunday**" (Мы встретимся в **воскресенье**.).
It refers to the day of the week following Saturday. You can also learn all the days of the week, months and seasons in the Quizlet bonus module

воскресенье

Sunday

врач | vrach

Part of speech: noun

Gender: masculine

Doctor, as in "The **doctor** examined the patient" (**Врач** осмотрел пациента.).
It refers to a medical professional who diagnoses and treats illnesses.

врач

doctor

время | врémya

Part of speech: noun

Gender: neuter

Time, as in "I don't have enough **time** to finish the project" (У меня нет достаточно **времени**, чтобы закончить проект.). It is a noun and is often used to describe the ongoing sequence of events or the duration in which things happen.

время

time

время года | vrémya góda

Part of speech: noun phrase

Gender: neuter

Season, as in "Spring is my favorite **season**" (Весна — моё любимое **время года**.).
It refers to one of the four periods of the year (spring, summer, autumn, winter) characterized by specific weather conditions and daylight hours.

время года

season

все | vse

Part of speech: pronoun

All, as in "**All** the books are on the table" (**Все** книги на столе.).
It refers to the entirety of a group or collection.

все

all, everyone

всегда | vsegdá

Part of speech: adverb

Always, as in "He **always** tells the truth" (Он **всегда** говорит правду.). It indicates that something occurs at all times or on every occasion without exception.

всегда

always

вторник | vtórnik

Part of speech: noun

Gender: masculine

Tuesday, as in "We have a meeting on **Tuesday**" (У нас встреча во **вторник**.). It refers to the second day of the week according to the traditional calendar.

вторник

Tuesday

входной билет | vkhodnóy bilét

Part of speech: noun

Gender: masculine

Admission ticket, as in "I bought an **admission ticket** to the museum" (Я купил **входной билет** в музей.). It is a noun and is often used to refer to a ticket required for entry.

входной билет

admission ticket

вчера | vcherá

Part of speech: adverb

Yesterday, as in "**Yesterday** was a sunny day" (**Вчера** был солнечный день.). It refers to the day before today.

вчера

yesterday

вчера вечером | vcherá vécherom

Part of speech: adverbial phrase

Last night, as in "**Last night** we watched a movie" (**Вчера вечером** мы смотрели фильм.). It refers to the evening or night of the previous day.

вчера вечером

last night

въезд | vyeźd

Gender: masculine

Part of speech: noun

Entrance, as in "The **entrance** to the parking lot is on the left" (**Въезд** на парковку находится слева.). It refers to a place where vehicles can enter an area.

въезд

entrance (for cars)

вы | vý

Part of speech: pronoun

You, as in "**You** are welcome to join us" (**Вы** можете присоединиться к нам.). It is used as a formal or plural form of addressing someone.

вы

you (plural)

выезд | výyezd

Gender: masculine

Part of speech: noun

Exit, as in "The **exit** from the highway is just ahead" (**Выезд** с шоссе находится прямо впереди.). It refers to a place where vehicles can leave an area.

выезд

exit

выходные | vykhodńye

Part of Speech: noun

Gender: plural

Weekend, as in "I love spending time with my family on the **weekend**" (Я люблю проводить время с семьёй на **выходных**.). It is a noun and is often used to refer to the days of rest at the end of the week.

выходные

weekend

газированная вода | sparkling water

Part of speech: noun

Gender: feminine

Sparkling water, as in "I prefer **sparkling water** over still water" (Я предпочитаю **газированную воду** обычной воде.). It is a noun and is often used to refer to water that has been carbonated with carbon dioxide gas.

газированная вода

sparkling water

гандбол | gandból

Part of speech: noun

Handball, as in "He plays **handball** every Saturday" (Он играет в **гандбол** каждую субботу.). It is a noun and is often used to refer to the sport played with a ball and goals.

гандбол

handball

где | gde

Part of speech: adverb

Where, as in "**Where** is the nearest store?" (**Где** находится ближайший магазин?). It is an adverb and is often used to ask about the location of something.

где

where

где-то | gde-tó

Part of speech: adverb

Somewhere, as in "I left my keys **somewhere** in the house" (Я оставил свои ключи **где-то** в доме.).
It is an adverb and is often used to indicate an unspecified or unknown location.

где-то

somewhere

гид | gíd

Gender: masculine

Part of speech: noun

Guide, as in "The **guide** showed us around the museum" (**Гид** показал нам музей.).
It is a noun and is often used to refer to a person who leads or directs others on a journey or tour.

гид

guide

глаз | glaz

Gender: masculine

Part of speech: noun

Eye, as in "She has beautiful blue **eyes**" (У неё красивые голубые **глаза**.).
It is a noun and is often used to refer to the organ of sight in humans and animals.

глаз

eye

глубокий | glubókij

Part of speech: adjective

Deep, as in "The lake is very **deep**" (Озеро очень **глубокое**.). It is an adjective and is often used to describe something that has a large distance from the top or surface to the bottom.

глубокий

deep

глупый | glúpij

Part of speech: adjective

Stupid, as in "It was a **stupid** mistake" (Это была **глупая** ошибка.). It is an adjective and is often used to describe someone or something lacking intelligence or common sense.

глупый

stupid, foolish

говорить | govoriť

Part of speech: verb
Verb group: -ить

Perfective: сказать | skazáť

Speak, as in "She likes **to speak** in public" (Она любит **говорить** на публике.). It is a verb and is often used to describe the act of conveying information or expressing thoughts verbally.

говорить

to speak, to talk

говядина | govyádina

Part of speech: noun

Gender: feminine

Beef, as in "I bought some **beef** for dinner" (Я купил **говядину** на ужин.).
It is a noun and is often used to refer to the meat from cattle.

говядина

beef

год | god

Part of speech: noun

Gender: masculine

Year, as in "This **year** has been very eventful" (Этот **год** был очень насыщенным.).
It is a noun and is often used to refer to a period of twelve months.

год

year

голова | golová

Part of speech: noun

Gender: feminine

Head, as in "He nodded his **head** in agreement" (Он кивнул **головой** в знак согласия.). It is a noun and is often used to refer to the upper part of the human body or the front part of an animal's body, containing the brain, eyes, ears, nose, and mouth.

голова

head

голодный | golódnyj

Part of speech: adjective

Hungry, as in "After the long walk, I was very **hungry**" (После долгой прогулки я был очень **голодный**.). It is an adjective and is often used to describe the feeling of needing or wanting food.

голодный

hungry

гольф | golf

Part of speech: noun

Gender: masculine

Golf, as in "He enjoys playing **golf** on weekends" (Он любит играть в **гольф** по выходным.). It is a noun and is often used to refer to the sport in which players use clubs to hit balls into a series of holes on a course in as few strokes as possible.

гольф

golf

гора | gorá

Part of speech: noun

Gender: feminine

Mountain, as in "They climbed the **mountain** to see the sunrise" (Они взобрались на **гору**, чтобы увидеть восход солнца.). It is a noun and is often used to refer to a large natural elevation of the earth's surface rising abruptly from the surrounding level.

гора

mountain

гордый | górodyj

Part of speech: adjective

Proud, as in "He was **proud** of his son" (Он был **горд** своим сыном.). It is an adjective and is often used to describe a feeling of deep pleasure or satisfaction derived from one's own achievements, the achievements of those with whom one is closely associated, or from qualities or possessions that are widely admired.

гордый

proud

город | górod

Part of speech: noun

Gender: masculine

City, as in "Moscow is a large **city**" (Москва — большой **город**.). It is a noun and is often used to refer to a large and significant town or urban area, typically one with a dense population and various infrastructures.

город

city

горький | gór'kij

Part of speech: adjective

Bitter, as in "The medicine tasted **bitter**" (Лекарство было **горьким** на вкус.). It is an adjective and is often used to describe a sharp, pungent taste or smell; it can also refer to a feeling of resentment or disappointment.

горький

bitter

горячий | goryáchij

Part of speech: adjective

Hot, as in "The soup is **hot**" (Суп **горячий**.). It is an adjective and is often used to describe something having a high temperature or something that causes a burning sensation.

горячий

hot

гостиница | gostínitsa

Part of speech: noun

Gender: feminine

Hotel, as in "We stayed at a nice **hotel**" (Мы остановились в хорошей **гостинице**.).
It is a noun and is often used to refer to an establishment providing accommodations, meals, and other services for travelers and tourists.

гостиница

hotel

гость | gost'

Part of speech: noun

Gender: masculine

Guest, as in "We have a **guest** coming for dinner" (У нас будет **гость** на ужин.). It is a noun and is often used to refer to a person who is invited to visit someone's home or attend an event.

гость

guest

готовить | bezháť

Part of speech: verb
Verb group: -ить

Perfective: приготовить | prigotovít'

Cook, as in "She likes to **cook** dinner every evening" (Она любит **готовить** ужин каждый вечер.).
It is a verb and is often used to describe the act of preparing food by combining, mixing, and heating ingredients.

готовить

to cook

град | grad

Part of speech: noun

Gender: masculine

Hail, as in "The **hail** damaged the car" (**Град** повредил машину.). It is a noun and is often used to describe small balls or lumps of ice that fall from the sky during a storm.

град

hail

градус | gráduc

Part of speech: noun

Gender: masculine

Degree, as in "The temperature is twenty **degrees**" (Температура двадцать **градусов**.).
It is a noun and is often used to describe a unit of measurement for temperature or angles.

градус

degree

граница | granítsa

Part of speech: noun

Gender: feminine

Border, as in "We crossed the **border** into another country" (Мы пересекли **границу** в другую страну.). It is a noun and is often used to describe the line separating two countries, states, or areas.

граница

border

гроза | grozá

Part of speech: noun

Gender: feminine

Thunderstorm, as in "A **thunderstorm** is approaching" (**Гроза** приближается.). It is a noun and is often used to describe a storm with thunder, lightning, and typically heavy rain or hail.

гроза

thunderstorm

гром | grom

Part of speech: noun

Gender: masculine

Thunder, as in "The **thunder** was so loud it shook the windows" (**Гром** был такой громкий, что окна задрожали.). It is a noun used to describe the sound caused by lightning during a storm.

гром

thunder

громкий | grómkiy

Part of Speech: adjective

Loud, as in "The music was too **loud**" (Музыка была слишком **громкой.**). It is an adjective used to describe a high volume of sound.

громкий

loud

грудь | grud'

Part of Speech: noun

Gender: feminine

Chest, as in "He felt pain in his **chest**" (Он почувствовал боль в **груди.**). It is a noun and is often used to describe the front part of the body between the neck and the abdomen.

грудь

chest, breast

грустный | grústnyy

Part of speech: adjective

Sad, as in "She felt **sad** after watching the movie" (Она почувствовала себя **грустной** после просмотра фильма.). It is an adjective and is often used to describe a feeling of unhappiness or sorrow.

грустный

sad

грязный | gryáznyy

Part of speech: adjective

Dirty, as in "The floor is **dirty** and needs cleaning" (Пол **грязный** и нуждается в уборке.). It is an adjective used to describe something that is unclean or covered with dirt.

грязный

dirty

да | da

Part of Speech: particle

Yes, as in "**Yes**, I agree with you" (**Да**, я с тобой согласен.). It is a particle used to express agreement or affirmation.

да

yes

давать | davát' (Imperfective)

Part of speech: verb
Verb group: -ать

Perfective: дать | dat'

Give, as in "I **give** my friend a book" (Я **даю** своему другу книгу.). It is a verb and used to describe the act of providing something to someone.

давать

to give

дайвинг | dájving

Part of speech: noun

Gender: masculine

Diving, as in "**Diving** is an exciting sport" (**Дайвинг** — это захватывающий спорт.). It is a noun and used to describe the activity of exploring underwater environments.

дайвинг

diving

два| dvá

Part of speech: numeral

Two, as in "I have **two** cats" (У меня **два** кота.). It is a numeral and used to indicate the quantity of two.

два

two

двадцать | dvádcat'

Part of speech: numeral

Twenty, as in "There are **twenty** students in the class" (В классе **двадцать** учеников.).
It is a numeral and used to indicate the quantity of twenty.

двадцать

twenty

двадцать восемь | dvádcat' vósem'

Part of speech: numeral

Twenty-eight, as in "She is **twenty-eight** years old" (Ей **двадцать восемь** лет.).
It is a numeral and used to indicate the quantity of twenty-eight.

двадцать восемь

twenty-eight

двадцать два | dvádcat' dvá

Part of speech: numeral

Twenty-two, as in "He has **twenty-two** books" (У него **двадцать два** книги.).
It is a numeral and used to indicate the quantity of twenty-two.

двадцать два

twenty-two

двадцать девять | dvádcat' dévjat'

Part of speech: numeral

Twenty-nine, as in "There are **twenty-nine** days in February during a leap year"
(В феврале **двадцать девять** дней в високосный год.). It is a numeral
and used to indicate the quantity of twenty-nine.

двадцать девять

twenty-nine

двадцать один | dvádcat' odín

Part of speech: numeral

Twenty-one, as in "He is **twenty-one** years old" (Ему **двадцать один** год.).
It is a numeral and is often used to indicate the quantity of twenty-one.

двадцать один

twenty-one

двадцать пять | dvádcat' pjat'

Part of speech: numeral

Twenty-five, as in "She has **twenty-five** apples" (У неё **двадцать пять** яблок.).
It is a numeral and is often used to indicate the quantity of twenty-five.

двадцать пять

twenty-five

двадцать семь | dvádcat' sém'

Part of speech: numeral

Twenty-seven, as in "She is **twenty-seven** years old" (Ей **двадцать семь**
лет.). It is a numeral used to represent the number 27.

двадцать семь

twenty-seven

двадцать три | dvádcat' trí

Part of speech: numeral

Twenty-three, as in "She read **twenty-three** books last year" (Она прочитала
двадцать три книги в прошлом году.). It is a numeral and used to indicate
the quantity of twenty-three.

двадцать три

twenty-three

двадцать четыре | dvádcat' chetýre

Twenty-four, as in "The store is open **twenty-four** hours" (Магазин открыт **двадцать четыре** часа.). It is a numeral and is often used to indicate the quantity of twenty-four.

двадцать четыре

twenty-four

двадцать шесть | dvádcat' shest'

Twenty-six, as in "He ran **twenty-six** miles" (Он пробежал **двадцать шесть** миль.).
It is a numeral and is often used to indicate the quantity of twenty-six.

двадцать шесть

twenty-six

двенадцать | dvenádcat'

Twelve, as in "There are **twelve** months in a year" (В году **двенадцать** месяцев.).
It is a numeral and is often used to indicate the quantity of twelve.

двенадцать

twelve

дверь | dver'

Gender: feminine

Door, as in "Please close the **door**" (Пожалуйста, закрой **дверь**.).
It refers to a movable barrier used to cover an opening, typically in a wall.

дверь

door

двести | dvésti

Part of speech: numeral

Two hundred, as in "The book costs **two hundred** rubles" (Книга стоит **двести** рублей.). It is a numeral used to indicate the quantity of two hundred.

двести

two hundred

девяносто | devyanósto

Part of speech: numeral

Ninety, as in "There are **ninety** students in the auditorium" (В аудитории **девяносто** студентов.). It is a numeral used to indicate the quantity of ninety.

девяносто

ninety

девятнадцать | devyatnádcat'

Part of speech: numeral

Nineteen, as in "She is **nineteen** years old" (Ей **девятнадцать** лет.).
It is a numeral used to indicate the quantity of nineteen.

девятнадцать

nineteen

девять | dévyat'

Part of speech: numeral

Nine, as in "There are **nine** apples on the table" (На столе **девять** яблок.).
It is a numeral used to indicate the quantity of nine.

девять

nine

девятьсот | dévyatsot

Part of speech: numeral

Nine hundred, as in "The car costs **nine hundred** dollars" (Машина стоит **девятьсот** долларов.). It is a numeral used to indicate the quantity of nine hundred

девятьсот

nine hundred

действительно | deystvítel'no

Part of speech: adverb

Really, as in "It is **really** important to understand this concept" (Это **действительно** важно понять этот концепт.). It is used to emphasize the truth or reality of a statement.

действительно

really, truly

делать | délat'

Part of speech: verb
Verb group: -ать

Perfective: сделать | zdélat'

To do, as in "I need **to do** my homework" (Мне нужно **делать** домашнее задание.). It is a verb and is used to describe the action of performing a task or creating something.

делать

to do, to make

день | dén'

Part of speech: noun

Gender: masculine

Day, as in "Today is a sunny **day**" (Сегодня солнечный **день**.). It is a noun and is often used to refer to a 24-hour period.

день

day

деньги | dén'gi

Part of speech: noun

Gender: feminine

Money, as in "I need **money** to buy groceries" (Мне нужны **деньги**, чтобы купить продукты.). It is a noun and is often used to refer to currency or financial resources.

деньги

money

деревня | bezháť

Part of speech: noun

Gender: feminine

Village, as in "She lives in a small **village**" (Она живет в маленькой **деревне.**).
It is a noun and is often used to describe a small rural community.

деревня

village

дерево | dér'evo

Part of speech: noun

Gender: neuter

Tree, as in "The **tree** is very tall" (**Дерево** очень высокое.). It is a noun and is often used to describe a large plant with a trunk and branches.

дерево

tree

десерт | desért

Part of speech: noun

Gender: masculine

Dessert, as in "I would like some **dessert** after dinner" (Я бы хотел **десерт** после ужина.).
It is a noun and is often used to refer to a sweet course served at the end of a meal.

десерт

dessert

десятилетие | desyatilétiye

Part of speech: noun

Gender: neuter

Decade, as in "A lot can change in a **decade**" (Многое может измениться за **десятилетие**.). It is a noun and is often used to refer to a period of ten years.

десятилетие

decade

десять | désyat'

Part of speech: numeral

Ten, as in "I have **ten** apples" (У меня **десять** яблок.).
It is a numeral used to represent the number 10.

десять

ten

десять тысяч | désyat' tysiach

Part of speech: numeral phrase

Ten thousand, as in "The stadium can hold **ten thousand** people" (Стадион может вместить **десять тысяч** человек.). It is a numeral phrase used to represent the number 10,000.

десять тысяч

ten thousand

дешевый | deshévy

Part of speech: adjective

Cheap, as in "This is a **cheap** product" (Это **дешевый** продукт.).
It is an adjective used to describe something that is low in price or cost.

дешевый

cheap

дизайнер | dizáyner

Part of speech: noun

Gender: masculine

Designer, as in "She is a talented fashion **designer**" (Она талантливый **дизайнер** моды.).
It is a noun used to refer to a person who plans and creates designs, such as in fashion, graphics, or interior design.

дизайнер

designer

длинный | dlínnyy

Part of speech: adjective

Long, as in "He has **long** hair" (У него **длинные** волосы.). It is an adjective used to describe something that has a great length or duration.

длинный

long

до | do

Part of speech: preposition

Up to, as in "The library is open **up to** 8 PM on weekdays" (Библиотека открыта **до** 8 вечера по будням.). It is a preposition and is often used to indicate a limit or maximum point in time or space.

до

up to

до полудня | do poludnya

Part of speech: noun

Gender: masculine

Forenoon, as in "I have a meeting scheduled for the **forenoon**" (У меня запланирована встреча на **до полудня**.). It is a noun and is often used to describe the period of the day between morning and noon.

до полудня

forenoon

дождливо | dozhdlivó

Part of speech: adverb

Rainy, as in "It is **rainy** today" (Сегодня **дождливо**.). It is an adverb and is often used to describe weather conditions.

дождливо

rainy

дождь | dózhd'

Gender: masculine

Part of speech: noun

Rain, as in "The **rain** is heavy today" (Сегодня сильный **дождь**.). It is a noun and is often used to describe precipitation.

дождь

rain

долина | doliná

Gender: feminine

Part of speech: noun

Valley, as in "The **valley** is surrounded by mountains" (**Долина** окружена горами.). It is a noun and is often used to describe a low area of land between hills or mountains.

долина

valley

дом | dóm

Gender: masculine

Part of speech: noun

House, as in "The **house** is big and beautiful" (**Дом** большой и красивый.). It is a noun and is often used to describe a building for human habitation.

дом

house

дорогой | dorogóy

Part of speech: adjective

Expensive, as in "This watch is very **expensive**" (Эти часы очень **дорогие.**).
It is an adjective and is often used to describe something that costs a lot of money.

дорогой

expensive

дорожная сумка | dorózhnaya súmka

Part of speech: noun

Gender: feminine

Travel bag, as in "I packed my clothes in a **travel bag**" (Я упаковал одежду в **дорожную сумку.**).
It is a noun and is often used to describe a bag used for carrying personal items during travel.

дорожная сумка

travel bag

достопримечательность | dostoprimechátnost'

Part of speech: noun

Gender: feminine

Attraction, as in "The museum is a popular **attraction** for tourists" (Музей — популярная **достопримечательность** для туристов.). It is a noun and is often used to describe a place that draws visitors due to its cultural, historical, or natural significance.

достопримечательность

attraction, landmark

дочь | doch'

Part of speech: noun

Gender: feminine

Daughter, as in "Her **daughter** is studying at the university" (Её **дочь** учится в университете.).
It is a noun and is used to refer to a female child in relation to her parents.

дочь

daughter

друг | droog

Gender: masculine

Part of speech: noun

Friend, as in "He is my best **friend**" (Он мой лучший **друг.**). It is a noun and is used to refer to a person with whom one has a bond of mutual affection.

друг

friend

дружелюбный | druzhelyúbnyy

Part of speech: adjective

Friendly, as in "She has a **friendly** smile" (У неё **дружелюбная** улыбка.). It is an adjective used to describe someone who is kind, pleasant, and easy to get along with.

дружелюбный

friendly

думать | dúmat' (Imperfective)

Perfective: подумать | podúmat'

Part of speech: verb
Verb group: -ать

Think, as in "I need **to think** about this decision" (Мне нужно **подумать** об этом решении.). It is a verb and is often used to describe the process of considering or reasoning about something.

думать

to think

еда | yedá

Gender: feminine

Part of speech: noun

Food, as in "The **food** is delicious" (**Еда** вкусная.). It is a noun and is often used to refer to any nutritious substance that people or animals eat or drink to maintain life and growth.

еда

food

едва | yedvá

Part of speech: adverb

Barely, as in "He **barely** managed to catch the train" (Он **едва** успел на поезд.).
It is an adverb and is often used to indicate that something is almost not the case or is achieved with great difficulty.

едва

barely

если | yésli

Part of speech: conjunction

If, as in "**If** it rains, we will stay home" (**Если** пойдет дождь, мы останемся дома.).
It is a conjunction and is often used to introduce a conditional clause, indicating a possibility or hypothetical situation.

если

if

есть | yest' (Imperfective)

Part of speech: verb
Verb group: irregular

Perfective: съесть | syest'

To eat, as in "I want **to eat** an apple" (Я хочу **съесть** яблоко.).
It is a verb and is often used to describe the act of consuming food.

есть

to eat

ехать | yéhat' (Imperfective)

Part of speech: verb
Verb group: irregular

Perfective: поехать | poéhat'

Go, as in "I plan **to go** to the city tomorrow" (Я планирую **ехать** в город завтра.).
It is a verb and is often used to describe traveling or moving from one place to another by means of a vehicle.

ехать

to go

ещё не | yeshchó ne

Part of speech: adverbial phrase

Not yet, as in "I have **not yet** finished my homework" (Я **ещё не** закончил домашнее задание.).
It is an adverbial phrase and is often used to indicate that something has not happened up to the present time but is expected to happen in the future.

ещё не

not yet

жаждущий | zházhdushchiy

Part of speech: adjective

Thirsty, as in "The traveler was **thirsty** after the long journey" (Путешественник был **жаждущий** после долгого пути.). It is an adjective and is often used to describe someone who needs or desires a drink.

жаждущий

thirsty, eager

ждать | zhdat' (Imperfective)

Part of speech: verb
Verb group: -ать

Perfective: захотеть | zakhotét'

to wait, as in "I will **wait** for you at the station" (Я буду **ждать** тебя на станции.).
It is a verb and is often used to describe the action of staying in one place until a particular time or event occurs.

ждать

to wait

желудок | zheludok

Part of speech: noun

Gender: masculine

Stomach, as in "He has a pain in his **stomach**" (У него болит **желудок**.).
It is a noun used to refer to the organ in the body where digestion begins.

желудок

stomach (organ)

жениться | zhenít'sya (Imperfective)

Part of speech: verb
Verb group: -иться

Perfective: пожениться | po-zhe-ní-t'sya

Marry, as in "He decided **to marry** his long-time girlfriend" (Он решил **жениться** на своей давней подруге.). It is a verb and is often used to describe the act of a man getting married.

жениться

to marry

женщина | zhénshchina

Part of speech: noun

Gender: feminine

Woman, as in "The **woman** is reading a book" (**Женщина** читает книгу.).
It is a noun and is often used to refer to an adult female person.

женщина

woman

живот | zhivót

Part of speech: noun

Gender: masculine

Stomach, as in "My **stomach** hurts" (У меня болит **живот**.). It is a noun and is often used to describe the part of the body where digestion occurs.

живот

stomach, belly

жизнь | zhízn'

Part of speech: noun

Gender: feminine

Life, as in "**Life** is beautiful" (**Жизнь** прекрасна.). It is a noun and is often used to describe the existence or experience of being alive.

жизнь

life

жильё | zhil'yó

Part of speech: noun

Gender: neuter

Accommodation, as in "Finding suitable **accommodation** during the trip was easy" (Найти подходящее **жильё** во время поездки было легко.). It is a noun and is often used to describe a place where someone stays temporarily.

жильё

accommodation

жить | zhit' (Imperfective)

Part of speech: verb
Verb group: -ить

Perfective: прожить | prozhit'

Live, as in "They **live** in a big city" (Они **живут** в большом городе.). It is a verb and is often used to describe residing in a place.

жить

to live

за | za

Part of speech: preposition

Behind, as in "The cat is hiding **behind** the curtain" (Кошка прячется **за** занавеской.). It is a preposition and is often used to indicate position or support.

за

behind, for

забывать | zabývat' (Imperfective)

Part of speech: verb
Verb group: -ать

Perfective: забыть | zabýt'

Forget, as in "She tends **to forget** important dates" (Она склонна **забывать** важные даты.). It is a verb and is often used to describe failing to remember something.

забывать

to forget

завод | zavód

Gender: masculine

Part of speech: noun

Factory, as in "He works at a car **factory**" (Он работает на автомобильном **заводе**.).
It is a noun and is used to describe a place where goods are manufactured.

завод

factory

завтра | záftra

Part of speech: adverb

Tomorrow, as in "We will meet **tomorrow**" (Мы встретимся **завтра**.).
It is an adverb used to refer to the day after today.

завтра

tomorrow

завтрак | záftrak

Gender: masculine

Part of speech: noun

Breakfast, as in "I had eggs for **breakfast**" (Я ел яйца на **завтрак**.).
It is a noun used to describe the first meal of the day.

завтрак

breakfast

заказ | zakáz

Gender: masculine

Part of speech: noun

Order, as in "I placed an **order** for a new book" (Я сделал **заказ** на новую книгу.).
It is a noun used to describe a request for something to be made, supplied, or served.

заказ

order

заказывать | zakázyvat' (Imperfective)

Part of speech: verb
Verb group: -ать

Perfective: заказать | zakazát'

To order, as in "She likes **to order** food online" (Она любит **заказывать** еду онлайн.).
It is a verb used to describe the action of requesting something to be made, supplied, or served.

заказывать

to order

заканчивать | zakánchivat' (Imperfective)

Part of speech: verb
Verb group: -ать

Perfective: закончить | zakónchit'

End, as in "The meeting will **end** soon" (Встреча скоро **заканчивается**.). It is a
verb and is often used to describe bringing something to a conclusion or completion.

заканчивать

to end

закат | zakát

Part of speech: noun

Gender: masculine

Sunset, as in "We watched the **sunset** from the beach" (Мы смотрели **закат** с пляжа.).
It is a noun and is often used to describe the time in the evening when the sun disappears
below the horizon.

закат

sunset

закрывать | zakrývat' (Imperfective)

Part of speech: verb
Verb group: -ать

Perfective: закрыть | zakrýt'

Close, as in "Please **close** the door" (Пожалуйста, **закрой** дверь.). It is a verb and is
often used to describe the action of shutting something, such as a door or window.

закрывать

to close

закуска | zakúska

Part of speech: noun

Gender: feminine

Appetizer, as in "We ordered an **appetizer** before the main course" (Мы заказали **закуску** перед основным блюдом.). It is a noun and is often used to describe a small dish served before a meal to stimulate the appetite.

закуска

appetizer, snack

замерзать | zamyerzát' (Imperfective)

Part of speech: verb
Verb group: -ать

Perfective: замёрзнуть | zamjórznut'

Freeze, as in "The lake begins to **freeze** in winter" (Озеро начинает **замерзать** зимой.). It is a verb and is often used to describe the process of becoming frozen or turning into ice due to cold temperatures.

замерзать

to freeze

занятой | zanyatój

Part of speech: adjective

Busy, as in "She is always **busy** with work" (Она всегда **занята** работой.). It is an adjective and is often used to describe someone who has a lot of tasks or activities to do, leaving little free time.

занятой

busy

запястье | zapyást'ye

Part of speech: noun

Gender: neuter

Wrist, as in "He wore a watch on his **wrist**" (Он носил часы на **запястье**.). It is a noun and is often used to describe the joint connecting the hand to the forearm.

запястье

wrist

зарабатывать | zarabátyvat' (Imperfective)

Part of speech: verb
Verb group: -ать

Perfective: заработать | zarabotát'

Earn, as in "She works hard **to earn** a living" (Она усердно работает, чтобы **зарабатывать** на жизнь.). It is a verb and is often used to describe the act of receiving money in exchange for work or services.

зарабатывать

to earn

зарплата | zarpláta

Part of speech: noun

Gender: feminine

Salary, as in "He receives his **salary** at the end of the month" (Он получает **зарплату** в конце месяца.). It is a noun and is often used to describe the regular payment received by an employee for their work.

зарплата

salary, wages

застенчивый | zasténchivyy

Part of speech: adjective

Shy, as in "He is a **shy** boy who doesn't talk much" (Он **застенчивый** мальчик, который мало разговаривает.). It is an adjective and is often used to describe someone who is reserved or feels uncomfortable in social situations.

застенчивый

shy, timid

зачем | zachem

Part of speech: adverb

Why, as in "**Why** are you doing this?" (**Зачем** ты это делаешь?).
It is an adverb used to ask about the reason or purpose behind an action.

зачем

why

3

заявление | zayavléniye

Part of speech: noun

Gender: neuter

Application, as in "He submitted his **application** for the university scholarship before the deadline." (Он подал своё з**аявление** на университетскую стипендию до крайнего срока.). It is a noun used to describe a formal request or submission for something, often in written form.

заявление

application

ЗВОНИТЬ | zvonít'

Part of speech: verb
Verb group: -ить

Perfective: позвонить | позвонить

Call, as in "I **call** my friend every evening" (Я **звоню** своему другу каждый вечер.). It is a verb and is often used to describe making a phone call.

звонить

to call

здание | zdánie

Part of speech: noun

Gender: Neuter

Building, as in "The **building** is very tall" (**Здание** очень высокое.). It is a noun and is often used to describe a structure with walls and a roof.

здание

building

здесь | zdés'

Part of speech: adverb

Here, as in "I live **here**" (Я живу **здесь**.). It is an adverb and is often used to indicate a location or place.

здесь

here

здоровый | zdoróvyy

Part of speech: adjective

Healthy, as in "Eating vegetables is **healthy**" (Есть овощи — это **здорово**.). It is an adjective and is often used to describe someone or something in good physical condition.

здоровый

healthy

зима | zimá

Part of speech: noun

Gender: feminine

Winter, as in "**Winter** is my favorite season" (**Зима** — моё любимое время года.). It is a noun and is often used to describe the coldest season of the year.

зима

winter

зимний день | zímniy den'

Part of speech: noun phrase

Gender: masculine

Winter day, as in "A **winter day** can be very beautiful" (**Зимний день** может быть очень красивым.). It is a noun phrase and is often used to describe a day during the winter season.

зимний день

winter day

злой | zloy

Part of speech: adjective

Angry, as in "He was **angry** about the mistake" (Он был **зол** из-за ошибки.).
It is an adjective and is often used to describe someone who is feeling or showing anger.

злой

angry

знать | znat' (Imperfective)

Perfective: узнать | uznat'

Part of speech: verb
Verb group: -ать

To know, as in "I **know** the answer" (Я **знаю** ответ.). It is a verb and is often used to express having knowledge or awareness of something.

знать

to know

зуб | zub

Gender: masculine

Part of speech: noun

Tooth, as in "The child lost a **tooth**" (Ребёнок потерял **зуб.**). This sentence describes a common event in childhood when a baby tooth falls out.

зуб

tooth

и | i

Part of speech: conjunction

And, as in "I like tea **and** coffee" (Я люблю чай **и** кофе.). It is a conjunction used to connect words or phrases, indicating that they are to be taken together.

и

and

играть | igráть (Imperfective)

Perfective: сыграть | sygráть

Part of speech: verb
Verb group: -ать

Play, as in "Children love **to play** outside" (Дети любят **играть** на улице.). It is a verb and is often used to describe engaging in activities for enjoyment or recreation.

играть

to play

идёт дождь / дождить | dozhdit' (Imperfective)

Part of speech: verb
Verb group: -ить

Perfective: подождить | podozhdít'

Rain, as in "It **rains** often in autumn" (Осенью часто **дождит**.). It is a verb and is often used to describe the weather condition of rain. It is categorized under **и** because it is often learned as part of the phrase **идёт** дождь (it's raining, or it's starting to rain). The verb **идёт**, which means "it is coming" or "it goes," is commonly used with дождь in this expression.

дождить

to rain

идёт снег / снежить | snezhít' (Imperfective)

Part of speech: verb
Verb group: -ить

Perfective: поснежить | posnezhít'

Snow, as in "It **snows** heavily in winter" (Зимой сильно **снежит**.). It is a verb and is often used to describe the weather condition of snow. The same applies here as with the vocabulary above. снежить is often taught with **идёт (идёт снег)**, which is why we have categorized it with и.

снежить

to snow

идти | idtí (Imperfective)

Part of speech: verb
Verb group: irregular

Perfective: пойти | paytí

Go, as in "I **go** to school every day" (Я **иду** в школу каждый день.). It is a verb and is often used to describe the action of moving from one place to another.

идти

to go

извините | izvinité (Imperfective)

Part of speech: verb
Verb group: -ить

Perfective: извинить | izvinít'

Sorry, as in "**Sorry**, I didn't mean to interrupt" (**Извините**, я не хотел вас перебивать.). It is a verb and is often used to apologize for a mistake or interruption.

извините

sorry

или | íli

Part of speech: conjunction

Or, as in "Do you want tea **or** coffee?" (Вы хотите чай **или** кофе?).
It is a conjunction and is often used to present alternatives or choices.

или

or

иметь | imét' (Imperfective)

Perfective: получить | poluchít

Part of speech: verb
Verb group: -еть

Have, as in "I **have** a car" (Я **имею** машину.). It is a verb and is often used to indicate possession or ownership.

иметь

to have

иначе | ináche

Part of speech: adverb

Differently, as in "Try to think about the problem **differently**" (Попробуй подумать о проблеме **иначе**.). It is an adverb and is often used to suggest an alternative approach or method.

иначе

differently

инженер | inzhener

Gender: masculine

Part of speech: noun

Engineer, as in "He works as an **engineer** at the factory" (Он работает **инженером** на заводе.).
It is a noun and is often used to describe a person who designs, builds, or maintains engines, machines, or structures.

инженер

engineer

иногда | inogdá

Part of speech: adverb

Sometimes, as in "**Sometimes** I read books before bed" (**Иногда** я читаю книги перед сном.). It is an adverb and is often used to indicate occasional frequency.

иногда

sometimes

интересный | interesnýy

Part of speech: adjective

Interesting, as in "This book is very **interesting**" (Эта книга очень **интересная**.). It is an adjective and is often used to describe something that captures attention or arouses curiosity.

интересный

interesting

интернет | internét

Part of speech: noun

Gender: masculine

Internet, as in "I use the **internet** to find information" (Я использую **интернет**, чтобы найти информацию.). It is a noun and is often used to refer to the global network of computers.

интернет

internet

искать | iskát' (Imperfective)

Part of speech: verb
Verb group: -ать

Perfective: найти | naytí

Search, as in "I **search** for my keys every morning" (Я **ищу** свои ключи каждое утро.). It is a verb and is often used to describe the act of looking for something.

искать

to search

использовать | ispól'zovat' (Imperfective)

Perfective: использовать | ispól'zovat'

Part of speech: verb
Verb group: -овать
special subgroup of the -ать verb group

Use, as in "I **use** a computer for work" (Я **использую** компьютер для работы.). It is a verb and is often used to describe the action of utilizing something for a purpose. As you can see, imperfective and perfective are the same here, **использовать** can be used for both depending on the context.

использовать

to use

испуганный | ispúgannyj

Part of speech: adjective

Afraid, as in "The **afraid** cat hid under the bed" (**Испуганная** кошка спряталась под кроватью.). This adjective is used to describe someone or something that is experiencing fear or apprehension.

испуганный

afraid

каждый | kázhdyy

Part of speech: pronoun

Every, as in "**Every** student must complete the assignment" (**Каждый** студент должен выполнить задание.). It is a pronoun and is often used to refer to all members of a group individually.

каждый

every

как | kak

Part of speech: conjunction/adverb

How, as in "**How** do you solve this problem?" (**Как** ты решаешь эту проблему?).
It is an adverb and is often used to inquire about the manner or method of doing something.

как

how

Как далеко это? | Kak dalekó éto?

Part of speech: phrase

How far, as in "**How far is it** to the nearest station?" (**Как далеко до ближайшей станции?**). It is a phrase used to inquire about the distance to a particular location.

Как далеко это?

How far is it?

как долго | kak dólgo

Part of speech: phrase

How long, as in "**How long** will the meeting last?" (**Как долго** будет длиться встреча?).
It is a phrase used to inquire about the duration of an event or action.

как долго

how long

Как мне добраться до...? | Kak mne dobrát'sya do...?

Part of speech: phrase

How do I get to, as in "**How do I get** to the train station?" (**Как мне добраться до** вокзала?).
It is a phrase used to ask for directions to a specific location.

Как мне добраться до

How do I get to...?

как часто | kak chásto

Part of speech: phrase

How often, as in "**How often** do you exercise?" (**Как часто** ты занимаешься спортом?).
It is a phrase used to inquire about the frequency of an action or event.

как часто

how often

каменщик | kámen'shchik

Part of speech: noun

Gender: masculine

Bricklayer, as in "The **bricklayer** is constructing a new patio." (**Каменщик** строит новый внутренний дворик.). It is a noun and is often used to describe a skilled worker who lays bricks to build structures.

каменщик

bricklayer, mason

камера | kámera

Part of speech: noun

Gender: feminine

Camera, as in "The **camera** takes high-quality photos." (**Камера** делает фотографии высокого качества.). It is a noun and is often used to describe a device used for taking photographs or recording videos.

камера

camera

карта | kárta

Part of speech: noun

Gender: feminine

Map, as in "The **map** shows all the hiking trails." (**Карта** показывает все туристические тропы.). It is a noun and is often used to describe a visual representation of an area, showing geographic features, roads, and landmarks.

карта

map

картофель | kartófel'

Part of speech: noun

Gender: masculine

Potato, as in "**Potatoes** are a staple food in many countries" (**Картофель** — основной продукт питания во многих странах.). It is a noun used to refer to the starchy tuber commonly eaten as a vegetable.

картофель

potato

кафе | kafé

Part of speech: noun

Gender: neuter

Café, as in "We met at the **café** for coffee." (Мы встретились в **кафе** на кофе.). It is a noun and is often used to describe a small restaurant where you can buy drinks and simple meals.

кафе

café

квартира | kvartíra

Part of speech: noun

Gender: feminine

Apartment, as in "She lives in a spacious **apartment** in the city." (Она живёт в просторной **квартире** в городе.). It is a noun and is often used to describe a set of rooms forming a separate residence within a building.

квартира

apartment

кислый | kíslıy

Part of speech: adjective

Sour, as in "The lemon is very **sour**." (Лимон очень **кислый**.). It is an adjective and is often used to describe a taste that is sharp, acidic, or tangy.

кислый

sour

кисть | kist'

Part of speech: noun

Gender: feminine

Brush, as in "The artist held a **brush** in his hand" (Художник держал **кисть** в руке.). It is a noun and is often used to describe a tool used for painting or drawing.

кисть

brush

кишечник | kishéchnik

Part of speech: noun

Gender: masculine

Intestine, as in "The doctor examined the **intestine**." (Доктор осмотрел **кишечник**.).
It is a noun and is often used to describe a part of the digestive system in the body.

кишечник

intestine

клубника | klubníka

Part of speech: noun

Gender: feminine

Strawberry, as in "She picked a ripe **strawberry**." (Она сорвала спелую **клубнику**.). It is a
noun and is often used to describe a sweet, red fruit commonly eaten fresh or used in desserts.

клубника

strawberry

ключ | klyuch

Part of speech: noun

Gender: masculine

Key, as in "He lost the **key** to the door." (Он потерял **ключ** от двери.).
It is a noun and is often used to describe an object used to open locks.

ключ

key

книга | kníga

Part of speech: noun

Gender: feminine

Book, as in "She is reading a fascinating **book**." (Она читает увлекательную **книгу**.). It is a noun
and is often used to describe a set of written or printed pages, usually bound with a protective cover.

книга

book

когда | kogdá

Part of speech: conjunction / adverb

When, as in "**When** will you arrive?" (**Когда** ты приедешь?). It is a conjunction/adverb and is often used to ask about the time something will happen or to introduce a time-related clause.

когда

when

кожа | kózha

Part of speech: noun

Gender: feminine

Skin, as in "She has very sensitive **skin**." (У неё очень чувствительная **кожа**.).
It is a noun and is often used to describe the outer covering of the body.

кожа

skin, leather

коктейль | koktéyl'

Part of speech: noun

Gender: masculine

Cocktail, as in "She ordered a refreshing **cocktail** at the bar." (Она заказала освежающий **коктейль** в баре.). It is a noun and is often used to describe a mixed drink typically made with alcohol and various other ingredients like fruit juice or soda.

коктейль

cocktail

колбаса | kolbasá

Part of speech: noun

Gender: feminine

Sausage, as in "He sliced the **sausage** for breakfast." (Он нарезал **колбасу** на завтрак.). It is a noun and is often used to describe a type of meat product typically made from ground meat, spices, and other ingredients, encased in a skin.

колбаса

sausage

колено | koléno

Part of speech: noun

Gender: neuter

Knee, as in "She injured her **knee** while running." (Она повредила **колено** во время бега.). It is a noun and is often used to describe the joint between the thigh and the lower leg in humans.

колено

knee

коллега | kolléga

Part of speech: noun

Gender: masculine

Colleague, as in "He discussed the project with his **colleague**." (Он обсудил проект со своим **коллегой**.). It is a noun and is often used to describe a person with whom one works, typically in a professional or business setting.

коллега

colleague

кольцо | kol'tsó

Part of speech: noun

Gender: neuter

Roundabout, as in "The car entered the **roundabout** and took the second exit." (Машина въехала на **кольцо** и выехала на втором съезде.). It is a noun and is often used to describe a circular road junction where traffic moves in one direction around a central island.

кольцо

roundabout

команда | kománda

Part of speech: noun

Gender: feminine

Team, as in "Our **team** won the championship." (Наша **команда** выиграла чемпионат.). It is a noun and is often used to describe a group of people who work together towards a common goal, especially in sports or professional settings.

команда

team

комната | kómnata

Part of speech: noun

Gender: feminine

Room, as in "The **room** was filled with sunlight." (**Комната** была наполнена солнечным светом.). It is a noun and is often used to describe an enclosed space within a building, typically used for a specific purpose such as sleeping, living, or working.

комната

room

компания | kompánia

Part of speech: noun

Gender: feminine

Company, as in "She joined the **company**." (Она присоединилась к **компании**.).
It is a noun and is often used to describe a business organization that sells goods or services.

компания

company

конечно | konéchno

Part of speech: adverb

Of course, as in "**Of course**, I will help you." (**Конечно**, я помогу тебе.).
It is an adverb used to express agreement or affirmation.

конечно

of course, certainly

контракт | kontrákt

Part of speech: noun

Gender: masculine

Contract, as in "They signed the **contract** yesterday." (Они подписали **контракт** вчера.).
It is a noun and is often used to describe a formal agreement between two or more parties, especially one that is legally binding.

контракт

contract

корабль | korábl'

Part of speech: noun

Gender: masculine

Ship, as in "The **ship** sailed across the ocean." (**Корабль** пересек океан.).
It is a noun and is often used to describe a large watercraft that travels on the sea.

корабль

ship

короткий | korótkiy

Part of speech: adjective

Short, as in "He has **short** hair." (У него **короткие** волосы.). It is an
adjective used to describe something that has a small length or duration.

короткий

short

кость | kost'

Part of speech: noun

Gender: feminine

Bone, as in "The dog buried the **bone** in the yard." (Собака закопала **кость** во дворе.).
It is a noun and is often used to describe the rigid organs that form part of the
endoskeleton of vertebrates.

кость

bone

которая | kotóraya

Part of speech: pronoun

Which, as in "The book, **which** is on the table, is mine." (Книга, **которая** на столе, моя.).
It is used to introduce a relative clause, providing more information about a noun.

которая

which (f.)

которое |kotóroe

Part of speech: pronoun

Which, as in "The house, **which** is on the corner, is ours." (Дом, **которое** на углу, наш.).
It is used to introduce a relative clause, providing more information about a neuter noun.

которое

which (n.)

который | kotóryy

Part of speech: pronoun

Which, as in "The car, **which** is parked outside, is mine." (Машина, **которая** припаркована снаружи, моя.). It is used to introduce a relative clause, providing more information about a masculine noun.

который

which (m.)

кофе | kófe

Part of speech: noun

Gender: masculine

Coffee, as in "I drink **coffee** every morning." (Я пью **кофе** каждое утро.). It is a noun and is often used to describe a popular beverage made from roasted coffee beans.

кофе

coffee

кошка | kóshka

Part of speech: noun

Gender: feminine

Cat, as in "The **cat** is sleeping on the sofa." (**Кошка** спит на диване.). It is a noun and is often used to describe a small domesticated carnivorous mammal with soft fur, a short snout, and retractable claws.

кошка

cat

красивый | krasívy

Part of Speech: adjective

Beautiful, as in "She wore a **beautiful** dress." (Она надела **красивое** платье.). It is an adjective used to describe something that is pleasing to the senses or mind aesthetically.

красивый

beautiful

кричать | krichát'

Part of speech: verb
Verb group: -ать

Perfective: крикнуть | kríknut'

To shout, as in "He began **to shout** loudly." (Он начал громко **кричать**.). It is a verb used to describe the action of raising one's voice loudly, often in anger or excitement.

кричать

to shout, to scream

кровь | krov'

Part of speech: noun

Gender: feminine

Blood, as in "**Blood** is essential for life." (**Кровь** необходима для жизни.). It is a noun and is often used to describe the red liquid that circulates in the arteries and veins of humans and other vertebrates, carrying oxygen and nutrients to the tissues and removing carbon dioxide and other wastes.

кровь

blood

круглый | krúglyy

Part of Speech: adjective

Round, as in "The table is **round**." (Стол **круглый**.). It is an adjective used to describe something that is shaped like a circle or has a circular form.

круглый

round

кто | kto

Part of speech: pronoun

Who, as in "**Who** is there?" (**Кто** там?). It is a pronoun used to ask about the identity of a person or people.

кто

who

кто-то | kto-to

Part of speech: pronoun

Someone, as in "**Someone** is at the door." (**Кто-то** у двери.).
It is a pronoun used to refer to an unspecified person.

кто-то

someone, somebody

куда | kudá

Part of Speech: adverb

Where to, as in "**Where** are you going?" (**Куда** ты идёшь?). It is an adverb used to ask about the destination or direction of movement.

куда

where to

курица | kúritsa

Gender: feminine

Chicken, as in "The **chicken** is in the yard." (**Курица** во дворе.). It is a noun used to describe a domesticated bird kept for its eggs or meat.

курица

chicken

кухня | kúkhnya

Part of speech: noun

Gender: feminine

Kitchen, as in "The **kitchen** is clean." (**Кухня** чистая.). It is a noun used to describe a room or area where food is prepared and cooked.

кухня

kitchen

лапша | lapshá

Part of speech: noun

Gender: feminine

Noodles, as in "I cooked **noodles** for dinner." (Я приготовил **лапшу** на ужин.). It is a noun used to describe a type of food made from unleavened dough that is rolled flat and cut into long strips or strings.

лапша

noodles

лёгкая атлетика | lyóhkaya atlétika

Part of speech: noun phrase

Gender: feminine

Athletics, as in "She excels in **athletics**." (Она преуспевает в **лёгкой** атлетике.). It is a noun phrase used to describe a collection of sporting events that involve competitive running, jumping, throwing, and walking.

лёгкая атлетика

athletics

лёгкий | lyógkiy

Part of speech: adjective

Light, as in "This bag is **light**." (Эта сумка **лёгкая**.). It is an adjective used to describe something that has little weight.

лёгкий

light, easy

легко | legkó

Part of speech: adverb

Easily, as in "She solved the problem **easily**." (Она **легко** решила задачу.).
It is an adverb used to describe doing something with little effort or difficulty.

легко

easily

лёгкое | lyókoye

Part of speech: noun

Gender: neuter

Lung, as in "The doctor examined the **lung**." (Доктор осмотрел **лёгкое**.).
It refers to one of the two respiratory organs in the chest responsible for breathing.

лёгкое

lung

ленивый | lenívy

Part of speech: adjective

Lazy, as in "He is a **lazy** student." (Он **ленивый** студент.). It is an
adjective used to describe someone who is unwilling to work or use energy.

ленивый

lazy

летать | letáť (Imperfective)

Part of speech: verb
Verb group: -ать

Perfective: полететь | poletéť

Fly, as in "Birds **fly** in the sky" (Птицы **летают** в небе.). It is a verb
and is often used to describe the action of moving through the air.

летать

to fly

летний день | létniy den'

Part of speech: noun phrase

Gender: masculine

Summer day, as in "A **summer day** is perfect for a picnic" (**Летний день** идеален для пикника.). It is a noun phrase and is often used to describe a day during the summer season.

летний день

summer day

лето | léto

Part of speech: noun

Gender: neuter

Summer, as in "**Summer** is my favorite season" (**Лето** — моё любимое время года.).
It is a noun and is often used to refer to the warmest season of the year.

лето

summer

ли | li

Part of speech: conjunction

Whether, as in "I don't know **whether** he will come" (Я не знаю, придёт **ли** он.).
It is a conjunction and is often used to introduce indirect questions or express doubt.

ли

whether, if

лицо | litsó

Part of speech: noun

Gender: neuter

Face, as in "Her **face** was full of joy" (Её **лицо** было полно радости.).
It is a noun and is often used to refer to the front part of a person's head.

лицо

face

лоб | lob

Part of speech: noun

Gender: masculine

Forehead, as in "He wiped the sweat from his **forehead**" (Он вытер пот со **лба**.).
It is a noun and is often used to refer to the part of the face above the eyebrows.

лоб

forehead

лодыжка | lodýzhka

Part of speech: noun

Gender: feminine

Ankle, as in "She twisted her **ankle** while running" (Она подвернула **лодыжку**, когда бежала.). It is a noun and is often used to refer to the joint connecting the foot with the leg.

лодыжка

ankle

ложка | lózhka

Part of speech: noun

Gender: feminine

Spoon, as in "Please pass me the **spoon**" (Пожалуйста, передай мне **ложку**.).
It is a noun and is often used to refer to a utensil used for eating or serving food.

ложка

spoon

локоть | lókot'

Part of speech: noun

Gender: masculine

Elbow, as in "He rested his **elbow** on the table" (Он опёрся **локтем** на стол.). It is a noun and is often used to refer to the joint connecting the forearm and the upper arm.

локоть

elbow

лучше | lúchshe

Part of speech: adverb

Better, as in "She sings **better** than anyone else" (Она поёт **лучше** всех.). It is an adverb and is often used to compare the quality or degree of an action or state.

лучше

better

лыжный спорт | lýzhny sport

Part of speech: noun phrase

Gender: masculine

Skiing, as in "**Skiing** is a popular winter sport" (**Лыжный спорт** — популярный зимний вид спорта.). It refers to the sport or activity of gliding over snow on skis.

лыжный спорт

skiing

любить | lyubít' (Imperfective)

Part of speech: verb
Verb group: -ить

Perfective: полюбить | polyubít'

Love, as in "I **love** my family" (Я **люблю** свою семью.).
It is a verb and is often used to express affection for someone.

любить

to love, to like

любовь | lyubóv'

Part of speech: noun

Gender: feminine

Love, as in "**Love** is a powerful emotion" (**Любовь** — это сильное чувство.). It is a noun and is often used to describe a deep affection or attachment to someone or something.

любовь

love

любопытный | lyubopýtny

Curious, as in "The **curious** child asked many questions" (**Любопытный** ребёнок задавал много вопросов.). It is an adjective and is often used to describe someone who is eager to know or learn something.

любопытный

curious

магазин | magazín

Gender: masculine

Store, as in "I went to the **store** to buy groceries" (Я пошёл в **магазин**, чтобы купить продукты.). It is a noun and is often used to refer to a place where goods are sold.

магазин

store, shop

маленький | lyubopýtny

Small, as in "The **small** dog barked loudly" (**Маленькая** собака громко лаяла.). It is an adjective and is often used to describe something of a limited size or extent.

маленький

small, little

маляр | malyár

Gender: masculine

Painter, as in "The **painter** is working on the house" (**Маляр** работает над домом.). It is a noun and is often used to refer to a person whose job is painting buildings, walls, or other structures.

маляр

painter

марафон | marafón

Part of speech: noun

Gender: masculine

Marathon, as in "She trained for months to run the **marathon**" (Она тренировалась несколько месяцев, чтобы пробежать **марафон**.). It is a noun and is often used to describe a long-distance running race, typically 42.195 kilometers (26.219 miles) long.

марафон

marathon

масло | bezhát'

Part of speech: noun

Gender: neuter

Oil, as in "Add some **oil** to the pan" (Добавь немного **масла** в сковороду.).
It is a noun and is often used to refer to a liquid used for cooking or lubrication.

масло

oil

мать | mat'

Part of speech: noun

Gender: feminine

Mother, as in "My **mother** is a teacher" (Моя **мать** — учительница.).
It is a noun and is often used to refer to a female parent.

мать

mother

машина | mashína

Part of speech: noun

Gender: feminine

Car, as in "She drives a new **car**" (Она водит новую **машину**.). It is a noun and is often used to refer to a motor vehicle used for transportation.

машина

car

медленно | médlenno

Part of speech: adverb

Slowly, as in "He walks **slowly** down the street" (Он **медленно** идёт по улице.).
It is an adverb and is used to describe an action that is performed at a slow pace.

медленно

slowly

медленный | médlennyy

Part of speech: adjective

Slow, as in "The turtle is slow" (Черепаха медленная.). It is used as an
adjective to describe something that moves or operates at a low speed.

медленный

slow

медсестра | medsestrá

Part of speech: noun

Gender: feminine

Nurse, as in "The **nurse** is taking care of the patient" (**Медсестра** ухаживает за пациентом.).
It is a noun and is often used to refer to a healthcare professional who provides medical care and
assistance to patients.

медсестра

nurse

между | bezháť

Part of Speech: Preposition

Between, as in "The cat is sitting **between** the chairs" (Кошка сидит **между** стульями.). It is a
preposition and is often used to indicate a position or relationship involving two or more entities.

между

between

мелкий | mélkiy

Part of speech: adjective

Shallow, as in "The water is **shallow**" (Вода **мелкая**.). It is an adjective and is often used to describe a body of water that is not deep.

мелкий

shallow

менеджер | ménedzher

Part of speech: noun

Gender: masculine

Manager, as in "The **manager** is organizing the team" (**Менеджер** организует команду.). It is a noun and is often used to refer to a person responsible for controlling or administering an organization or group of staff.

менеджер

manager

меню | menyú

Part of speech: noun

Gender: neuter

Menu, as in "The **menu** offers a variety of dishes" (**Меню** предлагает разнообразие блюд.). It is a noun and is often used to refer to a list of food and drink items available at a restaurant or café.

меню

menu

месяц | mésyats

Part of speech: noun

Gender: masculine

Month, as in "January is the first **month** of the year" (Январь — первый **месяц** года.). It is a noun and is often used to refer to one of the twelve divisions of the calendar year.

месяц

month

метро | metró

Part of speech: noun

Gender: neuter

Subway, as in "I take the **subway** to work every day" (Я езжу на **метро** на работу каждый день.). It is a noun and is often used to refer to an underground urban railway system used for mass transit.

метро

subway, metro

механик | mekhánik

Part of speech: noun

Gender: masculine

Mechanic, as in "The **mechanic** repaired the car" (**Механик** починил машину.). It is a noun and is often used to refer to a person who repairs and maintains machinery, especially engines and vehicles.

механик

mechanic

миллион | bezháť

Part of speech: noun

Gender: masculine

Million, as in "The city has a population of over one **million**" (В городе население более одного **миллиона**.). It is a noun and is often used to refer to the number 1,000,000.

миллион

million

мимо | mímo

Part of speech: preposition / adverb

Past, as in "He walked **past** the house" (Он прошёл **мимо** дома.). It is used as a preposition or adverb to indicate movement in relation to a location, meaning to go by or alongside something without stopping.

мимо

past

минута | minúta

Part of speech: noun

Gender: feminine

Minute, as in "Please wait a **minute**" (Пожалуйста, подождите **минуту**.).
It is a noun and is often used to refer to a unit of time equal to 60 seconds.

минута

minute

миска | míska

Part of speech: noun

Gender: feminine

Bowl, as in "She poured soup into the **bowl**" (Она налила суп в **миску**.). It is a
noun and is often used to refer to a deep, round dish or basin used for food or liquid.

миска

bowl

мобильный телефон | mobíl'nyy telefón

Part of speech: noun phrase

Gender: masculine

Mobile phone, as in "I forgot my **mobile phone** at home" (Я забыл свой **мобильный телефон**
дома.). It is a noun phrase used to refer to a portable telephone that can make and receive calls
over a radio frequency link.

мобильный телефон

mobile phone

может быть | mózhet byt'

Part of speech: adverb

Maybe, as in "**Maybe** it will rain tomorrow" (**Может быть**, завтра
пойдёт дождь.). It is an adverb used to express uncertainty or possibility.

может быть

maybe, perhaps

мозг | mozg

Part of speech: noun

Gender: masculine

Brain, as in "The **brain** controls all body functions" (**Мозг** контролирует все функции организма.). It is a noun used to refer to the organ inside the skull that controls thought, memory, and other essential functions.

мозг

brain

молния | mólnia

Part of speech: noun

Gender: feminine

Lightning, as in "The **lightning** struck the tree" (**Молния** ударила в дерево.).
It refers to the natural electrical discharge in the atmosphere.

молния

lightning

молодой | molodóy

Part of speech: adjective

Young, as in "He is a **young** man" (Он **молодой** человек.). It is an adjective used to describe someone or something that has lived or existed for only a short time.

молодой

young

молоко | molokó

Part of speech: noun

Gender: neuter

Milk, as in "She drinks a glass of **milk** every morning" (Она пьёт стакан **молока** каждое утро.).
It is a noun used to refer to the white liquid produced by the mammary glands of mammals, commonly consumed as a beverage.

молоко

milk

море | móre

Part of speech: noun

Gender: neuter

Sea, as in "We spent our vacation by the **sea**" (Мы провели отпуск у **моря**.).
It is a noun used to refer to the large body of saltwater that covers most of the Earth's surface and surrounds its landmasses.

море

sea

мороженое | morózhenoe

Part of speech: noun

Gender: neuter

Ice cream, as in "She loves chocolate **ice cream**" (Она любит шоколадное **мороженое**.).
It is a noun used to refer to a sweet, frozen dessert made from or containing cream or milk and sugar, often flavored.

мороженое

ice cream

Москва | Moskvá

Part of speech: noun

Gender: feminine

Moscow, as in "**Moscow** is the capital of Russia" (**Москва** — столица России.).
It is a noun and is often used to refer to the capital city of Russia.

Москва

Moscow

мост | móst

Part of speech: noun

Gender: masculine

Bridge, as in "The **bridge** connects the two cities" (**Мост** соединяет два города.).
It is a noun and is often used to describe a structure built to span physical obstacles.

мост

bridge

мужчина | muzhchína

Part of speech: noun

Gender: masculine

Man, as in "The **man** is reading a book" (**Мужчина** читает книгу.).
It is a noun and is often used to refer to an adult male human.

мужчина

man

музей | muzéy

Part of speech: noun

Gender: masculine

Museum, as in "We visited the **museum** on Saturday" (Мы посетили **музей** в субботу.).
It is a noun and is often used to refer to a building where objects of historical, scientific, artistic, or cultural interest are stored and exhibited.

музей

museum

мы | bezhát'

Part of speech: pronoun

We, as in "**We** are going to the park" (**Мы** идём в парк.). It is a pronoun and is often used to refer to a group of people that includes the speaker.

мы

we

мыть | myt' (Imperfective)

Part of speech: verb
Verb group: -ить

Perfective: помыть | pomýt'

Wash, as in "I need **to wash** the dishes" (Мне нужно **помыть** посуду.). It is a verb and is often used to describe the action of cleaning something with water and, typically, soap.

мыть

to wash

мышца | mýshtsa

Part of speech: noun

Gender: feminine

Muscle, as in "He strained a **muscle** while lifting weights" (Он потянул **мышцу**, поднимая тяжести.). It is a noun and is often used to refer to a band or bundle of fibrous tissue in a human or animal body that has the ability to contract, producing movement in or maintaining the position of parts of the body.

мышца

muscle

мягкий | myáhkij

Part of speech: adjective

Soft, as in "The pillow is very **soft**" (Подушка очень **мягкая**.). It is an adjective and is often used to describe something that is easy to mold, cut, compress, or fold; not hard or firm to the touch.

мягкий

soft

мясо | myáso

Part of speech: noun

Gender: neuter

Meat, as in "She bought some **meat** for dinner" (Она купила **мясо** на ужин.). It is a noun and is often used to refer to the flesh of an animal (especially a mammal) as food.

мясо

meat

на восток | na vostók

Part of speech: prepositional phrase

To the east, as in "**To the east**, the sun rises" (**На восток** солнце встает.). It is a prepositional phrase and is often used to indicate direction or movement towards the east.

на восток

to the east

на запад | na západ

Part of speech: prepositional phrase

To the west, as in "We are traveling **to the west**" (Мы путешествуем **на запад**.). It is a prepositional phrase and is often used to indicate direction or movement towards the west.

на запад

to the west

на самом деле | na sámom déle

Part of speech: adverb

Actually, as in "**Actually**, I don't like coffee." (**На самом деле**, мне не нравится кофе.).
It is an adverb and is often used to express the true state of affairs or to correct a misconception.

на самом деле

actually, in fact

на север | na séver

Part of speech: prepositional phrase

North, as in "We are traveling to the **north**." (Мы едем **на север**.). It is a prepositional phrase and is often used to indicate direction towards the north.

на север

to the north

на этой неделе | na étoy nedéle

Part of speech: prepositional phrase

Week, as in "We will meet **this week**." (Мы встретимся **на этой неделе**.). It is a prepositional phrase and is often used to specify a time frame within the current week.

на этой неделе

this week

на юг | na yúg

Part of speech: prepositional phrase

South, as in "We are heading to the **south**." (Мы направляемся **на юг**.).
It is a prepositional phrase and is often used to indicate direction towards the south.

на юг

to the south

наверняка | navernyaká

Part of speech: adverb

Surely, as in "He will **surely** come to the party." (Он **наверняка** придет на вечеринку.).
It is an adverb and is often used to express certainty or strong likelihood.

наверняка

surely, certainly

наверху | naverkhú

Part of speech: adverb

Above, as in "The cat is sleeping **above** on the shelf" (Кот спит **наверху** на полке.). It is
an adverb and is often used to describe a location that is higher or above something else.

наверху

above, upstairs

надеяться | nadéyat'sya (Imperfective)

Part of speech: verb
Verb group: -еться

Perfective: понадеяться | ponadéyat'sya

Hope, as in "I **hope** to see you soon" (Я **надеюсь** скоро тебя увидеть.). It is a
verb and is often used to express a desire or expectation for something to happen.

надеяться

to hope

налево | nalévo

Part of speech: adverb

To the left, as in "Turn **to the left** at the next street" (Поверни **налево** на следующей улице.). It is an adverb and is often used to indicate direction.

налево

to the left

намеренно | namérenno

Part of speech: adverb

Deliberately, as in "He **deliberately** ignored the warning" (Он **намеренно** проигнорировал предупреждение.). It is an adverb and is often used to describe an action done on purpose or with intent.

намеренно

deliberately

напиток | napítok

Part of speech: noun

Gender: masculine

Drink, as in "I would like a cold **drink**" (Я бы хотел холодный **напиток**.).
It is a noun and is often used to refer to any liquid that can be consumed.

напиток

drink, beverage

направление | napravléniye

Part of speech: noun

Gender: neuter

Direction, as in "She asked for the direction to the museum" (Она спросила направление к музею.).
It is a noun and is often used to refer to the course or path on which something is moving or pointing.

направление

direction

направо | napravo

Part of speech: adverb

To the right, as in "Turn **to the right** at the corner" (Поверни **направо** на углу.).
It is an adverb and is often used to indicate direction.

направо

to the right

напротив | naprótiv

Part of speech: preposition / adverb

opposite, as in "The bank is **opposite** the supermarket" (Банк находится **напротив** супермаркета.).
It is a preposition/adverb and is used to describe a position directly facing or across from something.

напротив

opposite

настольный теннис | nastólny ténnis

Part of speech: noun

Gender: masculine

Table tennis, as in "We played **table tennis** all afternoon" (Мы играли в **настольный теннис** весь день.). It is a noun and is used to refer to the sport played on a table with small paddles and a lightweight ball.

настольный теннис

table tennis, ping pong

находить | nakhodít' (Imperfective)

Part of speech: verb
Verb group: -ить

Perfective: найти | naytí

Find, as in "I can't **find** my keys" (Я не могу **найти** свои ключи.). It is a verb and is often used to describe the action of discovering or locating something.

находить

to find

начальник | nachál'nik

Part of speech: noun

Gender: masculine

Boss, as in "My **boss** gave me a new project" (Мой **начальник** дал мне новый проект.).
It is a noun and is used to refer to a person in charge or a supervisor in a workplace.

начальник

boss, supervisor

начинать | nachinát' (Imperfective)

Part of speech: verb
Verb group: -ать

Perfective: начать | pobezhát'

Start, as in "**I start** my work at 9 AM" (Я **начинаю** работать в 9 утра.). It is a verb
and is often used to describe the action of commencing or initiating something.

начинать

to start, to begin

неважный | nevázhnyy

Part of speech: adjective

Unimportant, as in "This detail is **unimportant** to the overall plan" (Эта деталь **неважна**
для общего плана.). It is an adjective and is used to describe something that lacks
significance or importance.

неважный

unimportant

негазированная вода | egaziróvannaya vodá

Part of speech: noun phrase

Gender: feminine

Still water, as in "I prefer **still water** over sparkling water" (Я предпочитаю **негазированную
воду** газированной.). It is a noun phrase used to describe water that does not contain carbonation.

негазированная вода

still water

неделя | nedél'ya

Part of Speech: noun

Gender: feminine

Week, as in "I will finish the project next **week**" (Я закончу проект на следующей **неделе**.). It is a noun used to refer to a period of seven days.

неделя

week

недружелюбный | nedruzhelyúbnyy

Part of Speech: adjective

Unfriendly, as in "The new neighbor seemed **unfriendly** at first" (Новый сосед сначала показался **недружелюбным**.). It is an adjective used to describe someone or something that is not friendly or welcoming.

недружелюбный

unfriendly

некоторые | nékotorye

Part of speech: pronoun

Some, as in "**Some** people prefer tea over coffee" (**Некоторые** люди предпочитают чай кофе.). It is a pronoun used to refer to an unspecified number of people or things within a larger group.

некоторые

some

неловкий | nelóvkiy

Part of speech: adjective

Embarrassing, as in "It was an **embarrassing** moment when he forgot the words to his speech" (Это был **неловкий** момент, когда он забыл слова своей речи.). It is an adjective used to describe situations that cause discomfort or embarrassment.

неловкий

embarrassing

немедленно | nemédlenno

Immediately, as in "She responded **immediately** to the urgent request" (Она **немедленно** ответила на срочный запрос.). It is an adverb used to describe actions that are done without delay.

немедленно

immediately

неполный рабочий день | nepólnyy rabóchiy den'

Part-time, as in "She works **part-time** while attending university" (Она работает на **неполный рабочий день**, пока учится в университете.). This phrase is used to describe a work schedule that is less than full-time, typically involving fewer hours.

неполный рабочий день

part-time

неправильный | neprávil'nyy

Incorrect, as in "He gave an **incorrect** answer to the question" (Он дал **неправильный** ответ на вопрос.). It is an adjective used to describe something that is not correct or accurate.

неправильный

incorrect, wrong

непунктуальный | nepunktuálʹnyy

Unpunctual, as in "He is often **unpunctual**, arriving late to meetings" (Он часто **непунктуальный**, опаздывает на встречи.). This adjective is used to describe someone who does not arrive on time or is habitually late.

непунктуальный

unpunctual, tardy

нервы | nérvy

Part of speech: noun

Gender: masculine

Nerves, as in "Before the performance, her **nerves** were on edge" (Перед выступлением её **нервы** были на пределе.). This noun is used to describe the state of being anxious or tense, often in stressful situations.

нервы

nerves

несколько | néskol'ko

Part of speech: pronoun

Several, as in "I have **several** books to read" (У меня есть **несколько** книг для чтения.). This pronoun is used to indicate an indefinite, but small, number of items or people.

несколько

several, a few

нести | nestí (Imperfective)

Part of speech: verb
Verb group: irregular

Perfective: понести | ponestí

Carry, as in "She **carries** the bag to school every day" (Она **несёт** сумку в школу каждый день.). It is a verb and is used to describe the action of transporting something from one place to another.

нести

to carry

нет | nyét

Part of speech: adverb

No, as in "**No**, I don't want any tea" (**Нет**, я не хочу чая.). It is an adverb and is often used to express negation or refusal.

нет

no

нигде | nigdé

Part of speech: adverb

Nowhere, as in "I can find my keys **nowhere**" (Я **нигде** не могу найти свои ключи.).
It is an adverb and is often used to indicate the absence of a location or place.

нигде

nowhere

никогда | bezháť

Part of speech: adverb

Never, as in "I have **never** been to Paris" (Я **никогда** не был в Париже.). It is an
adverb and is often used to indicate that something has not happened at any time.

никогда

never

никто | niktó

Part of speech: pronoun

No one, as in "**No one** was at the party" (**Никто** не был на вечеринке.). It is a
pronoun and is often used to indicate that there are no people present or
involved.

никто

no one, nobody

ничего | nichyegó

Part of speech: pronoun

Nothing, as in "There is **nothing** in the box" (В коробке **ничего** нет.).
It is a pronoun and is often used to indicate the absence of anything.

ничего

nothing

НО | no

Part of speech: conjunction

But, as in "I wanted to go for a walk, **but** it started raining" (Я хотел пойти на прогулку, **но** начался дождь.). It is a conjunction used to introduce a contrast or exception.

но

but

НОВЫЙ | nóvyy

Part of speech: adjective

New, as in "I bought a **new** car" (Я купил **новую** машину.). It is an adjective used to describe something that has recently been made, created, or introduced.

новый

new

НОГА | nogá

Gender: feminine

Part of speech: noun

Leg, as in "She injured her **leg** while playing soccer" (Она повредила **ногу**, играя в футбол.). It is a noun used to refer to the limb of a person or animal used for walking or support.

нога

leg

НОЖ | nozh

Gender: masculine

Part of speech: noun

Knife, as in "He used a **knife** to cut the bread" (Он использовал **нож**, чтобы нарезать хлеб.). It is a noun used to refer to a tool with a sharp blade for cutting.

нож

knife

ноль | nol'

Part of speech: noun

Gender: masculine

Zero, as in "The temperature dropped to **zero** degrees" (Температура упала до **нуля** градусов.). It is a noun used to represent the number 0.

ноль

zero

нормально | normál'no

Part of speech: adverb

Normally, as in "Everything is going **normally**" (Всё идёт **нормально**.). It is an adverb used to describe something that is proceeding in a usual or expected manner.

нормально

normally

нос | nos

Part of speech: noun

Gender: masculine

Nose, as in "He has a cold and his **nose** is stuffy" (У него простуда, и **нос** заложен.). It is a noun used to refer to the part of the face that contains the nostrils and is used for breathing and smelling.

нос

nose

ночь | noch'

Part of speech: noun

Gender: feminine

Night, as in "The stars are visible at **night**" (Звёзды видны **ночью**.). It is a noun used to refer to the period of darkness between sunset and sunrise.

ночь

night

нуждаться | nuzhdát'sya (Imperfective)

Perfective: потребовать | potrebováť

Part of speech: verb
Verb group: -ать

Need, as in "I **need** help with my homework" (Я **нуждаюсь** в помощи с домашним заданием.). It is a verb and is often used to express a requirement or necessity for something.

нуждаться

to need

обед | obéd

Gender: masculine

Part of speech: noun

Lunch, as in "We have **lunch** at noon" (Мы **обедаем** в полдень.).
It is a noun and is often used to describe a meal in the middle of the day.

обед

lunch

облако | óblako

Gender: neuter

Part of speech: noun

Cloud, as in "The **cloud** is white and fluffy" (**Облако** белое и пушистое.). It is a noun and is often used to describe a visible mass of condensed water vapor floating in the sky.

облако

cloud

облачно | óblachno

Part of speech: adverb

Cloudy, as in "It is **cloudy** today" (Сегодня **облачно**.). It is an adverb and is often used to describe the weather condition when the sky is covered with clouds.

облачно

cloudy

обмен валюты | obmén valyúty

Part of speech: noun phrase

Gender: masculine

Currency exchange, as in "I need to find a **currency exchange**" (Мне нужно найти **обмен валюты**.). It is a noun phrase and is often used to refer to the process of exchanging one currency for another.

обмен валюты

currency exchange

объяснять | obyasnyát' (Imperfective)

Part of speech: verb
Verb group: -ять
special and rare verb group

Perfective: объяснить | obyasnít'

Explain, as in "The teacher **explains** the lesson clearly" (Учитель ясно **объясняет** урок.).
It is a verb and is often used to describe the act of making something clear or understandable.

объяснять

to explain

обычно | obýchno

Part of speech: adverb

Usually, as in "I **usually** wake up at 7 AM" (Я **обычно** просыпаюсь в 7 утра.).
It is an adverb and is often used to describe something that happens regularly or typically.

обычно

usually

обязательно | ob"yazátel'no

Part of speech: adverb

Necessarily, as in "You must **necessarily** wear a helmet when riding a bike" (Вы **обязательно** должны носить шлем при езде на велосипеде.). It is an adverb and is often used to emphasize that something is required or certain.

обязательно

necessarily, definitely

овощи | óvoshi

Part of speech: noun

Gender: masculine

Vegetables, as in "I eat **vegetables** every day" (Я ем **овощи** каждый день.).
It is a noun and is often used to refer to edible plants or parts of plants.

овощи

vegetables

огонь | ogón'

Part of speech: noun

Gender: masculine

Fire, as in "The **fire** kept us warm during the night" (**Огонь** согревал нас ночью.). It is a noun and is often used to describe the phenomenon of combustion that produces heat and light.

огонь

fire

один | odín

Part of Speech: numeral

One, as in "I have **one** book" (У меня есть **одна** книга.).
It is used as a numeral to indicate a single unit or item.

один

one

одиннадцать | odínnadtsat'

Part of Speech: numeral

Eleven, as in "There are **eleven** players on a soccer team" (В футбольной команде **одиннадцать** игроков.). It is used as a numeral to indicate the quantity of eleven.

одиннадцать

eleven

океан | okeán

Part of speech: noun

Gender: masculine

Ocean, as in "The **ocean** is vast and deep" (**Океан** огромен и глубок.). It is used to refer to the large bodies of saltwater that cover most of the Earth's surface.

океан

ocean

окно | oknó

Part of speech: noun

Gender: neuter

Window, as in "The **window** is open" (**Окно** открыто.). It is used to refer to an opening in a wall or roof of a building, typically fitted with glass, to admit light or air and allow people to see out.

окно

window

он | on

Part of speech: pronoun

Gender: masculine

He, as in "**He** is my friend" (**Он** мой друг.). It is used to refer to a male person or animal previously mentioned or easily identified.

он

he

она | oná

Part of speech: pronoun

Gender: feminine

She, as in "**She** is my sister" (**Она** моя сестра.). It is used to refer to a female person or animal previously mentioned or easily identified.

она

she

они | bezháť

Part of speech: pronoun

They, as in "**They** are my friends" (**Они** мои друзья.). It is used to refer to two or more people or things previously mentioned or easily identified, regardless of gender.

они

they

опасный | opásnyy

Part of speech: adjective

Dangerous, as in "This is a **dangerous** road" (Это **опасная** дорога.).
The adjective agrees in gender, number, and case with the noun it modifies.

опасный

dangerous

осенний день | osénniy den'

Part of speech: noun phrase

Gender: masculine

Autumn day, as in "An **autumn day** can be very beautiful" (**Осенний день** может быть очень красивым.). It is a noun phrase and is often used to describe a day during the autumn season.

осенний день

autumn day

осень | ósen'

Part of speech: noun

Gender: feminine

Autumn, as in "**Autumn** is my favorite season" (**Осень** — моё любимое время года.).
It is a noun and is often used to refer to the season between summer and winter.

осень

autumn

основное блюдо | osnovnóe blýdo

Part of speech: noun phrase

Gender: neuter

Main course, as in "The **main course** was delicious" (**Основное блюдо** было вкусным.). It is a noun phrase and is often used to refer to the primary dish in a meal.

основное блюдо

main course

особенно | osóbenno

Part of speech: adverb

Especially, as in "I love summer, **especially** the long days" (Я люблю лето, **особенно** длинные дни.). It is an adverb and is often used to emphasize a particular aspect or detail.

особенно

especially

оставаться | bezháť (Imperfective)

Part of speech: verb
Verb group: -ать

Perfective: остаться | ostát'sya

Stay, as in "I prefer **to stay** at home during the weekend" (Я предпочитаю **оставаться** дома на выходных.). It is a verb and is often used to describe staying in a place or condition.

оставаться

to stay

остановка | bezháť

Part of speech: noun

Gender: feminine

Stop, as in "The bus **stop** is near my house" (Автобусная **остановка** находится рядом с моим домом.). It is a noun and is often used to refer to a place where vehicles stop to pick up or drop off passengers.

остановка

stop (bus, tram)

осторожный | ostorózhnyy

Part of speech: adjective

Careful, as in "He is a very **careful** driver" (Он очень **осторожный** водитель.).
It is an adjective and is often used to describe someone who is cautious and avoids risks.

осторожный

careful, cautious

остров | óstrov

Part of speech: noun

Gender: masculine

Island, as in "We spent our vacation on a tropical **island**" (Мы провели отпуск на тропическом **острове**.). It is a noun and is used to refer to a piece of land surrounded by water.

остров

island

отвечать | otvechát' (Imperfective)

Part of speech: verb
Verb group: -ать

Perfective: ответить | otvétit'

Answer, as in "She likes **to answer** questions in class" (Она любит **отвечать** на вопросы в классе.). It is a verb used to describe the act of responding to a question or statement.

отвечать

to answer, to reply

отдельно | otdélno

Part of speech: adverb

Separately, as in "Please pack these items **separately**" (Пожалуйста, упакуйте эти вещи **отдельно**.). It is an adverb used to indicate that something is done or exists apart from others.

отдельно

separately, apart

отец | otéts

Part of speech: noun

Gender: masculine

Father, as in "My **father** is a doctor" (Мой **отец** — врач.).
It is a noun used to refer to a male parent.

отец

father

открывать | otkrývat' (Imperfective)

Part of speech: verb
Verb group: -ать

Perfective: открыть | otkrýt'

Open, as in "She likes to **open** the windows in the morning" (Она любит **открывать** окна по утрам.). It is a verb used to describe the action of making something accessible or removing a barrier.

открывать

to open

открытка | otkrýtka

Part of speech: noun

Gender: feminine

Postcard, as in "I sent a **postcard** from Paris" (Я отправил **открытку** из Парижа.). It is a noun used to refer to a card, often with a picture on one side, sent without an envelope.

открытка

postcard, greeting card

откуда | otkúda

Part of speech: adverb

From where, as in "**Where** are you from?" (**Откуда** ты?). It is an adverb used to ask or indicate the origin or source of something.

откуда

from where

отправлять | otpravlyát'

Perfective: отправить | otprávit'

Part of speech: verb
Verb group: -ать

Send, as in "I need **to send** a letter" (Мне нужно **отправлять** письмо.). It is a verb used to describe the action of causing something to go or be taken to a particular destination.

отправлять

to send, to dispatch

отпуск | ótpusk

Gender: masculine

Part of speech: noun

Vacation, as in "I am going on **vacation** next week" (Я уезжаю в **отпуск** на следующей неделе.). It is a noun used to refer to a period of time when someone is away from work, often for rest or travel.

отпуск

vacation, leave

офис | ófis

Gender: masculine

Part of speech: noun

Office, as in "She works in an **office** downtown" (Она работает в **офисе** в центре города.). It is a noun used to refer to a room or set of rooms where business, professional, or clerical work is conducted.

офис

office

официант | ofitsiánt

Gender: masculine

Part of speech: noun

Waiter, as in "The **waiter** took our order" (**Официант** принял наш заказ.). It is a noun used to refer to a person who serves food and drinks to customers in a restaurant.

официант

waiter

официантка | ofitsiántka

Part of speech: noun

Gender: feminine

Waitress, as in "The **waitress** brought our drinks" (**Официантка** принесла наши напитки.).
It is a noun used to refer to a female server who serves food and drinks to customers in a restaurant.

официантка

waitress

палец | pálets

Part of speech: noun

Gender: masculine

Finger, as in "He cut his **finger**" (Он порезал **палец**.). It is a noun used to refer to the digits on the hands or feet of a human or animal.

палец

finger

палец ноги | pálets nogí

Part of speech: noun phrase

Gender: masculine

Toe, as in "I stubbed my **toe**" (Я ударил **палец ноги**.).
This phrase is used to specifically refer to the digits on the foot.

палец ноги

toe

парикмахер | parikmáher

Part of speech: noun

Gender: masculine

Hairdresser, as in "The **hairdresser** cut my hair" (**Парикмахер** подстриг мне волосы.).
It is a noun used to refer to a person whose job is to cut, style, and color hair.

парикмахер

hairdresser, barber

парк | park

Part of speech: noun

Gender: masculine

Park, as in "We went for a walk in the **park**" (Мы пошли на прогулку в **парк**.).
It is a noun used to refer to a large public green area in a town, used for recreation.

парк

park

паром | paróm

Part of speech: noun

Gender: masculine

Ferry, as in "We took a **ferry** across the river" (Мы переправились через реку на **пароме**.). It is a noun used to refer to a boat or ship that carries people, vehicles, and goods across a body of water.

паром

ferry

парусный спорт | párusny sport

Part of speech: noun

Gender: masculine

Sailing, as in "**Sailing** is a popular sport in coastal areas" (**Парусный** спорт — популярный вид спорта в прибрежных районах.). It is a noun and is often used to describe the activity of navigating a boat using sails.

парусный спорт

sailing

паспорт | pásport

Part of speech: noun

Gender: masculine

Passport, as in "I need my **passport** to travel abroad" (Мне нужен **паспорт**, чтобы поехать за границу.). It is a noun and is often used to refer to an official document for international travel.

паспорт

passport

пассажир | passazhír

Part of speech: noun

Gender: masculine

Passenger, as in "The **passenger** boarded the train" (**Пассажир** сел на поезд.). It is a noun and is often used to describe a person traveling in a vehicle but not operating it.

пассажир

passenger

паста | pásta

Part of speech: noun

Gender: feminine

Pasta, as in "I cooked **pasta** for dinner" (Я приготовил **пасту** на ужин.). It is a noun and is often used to refer to a type of Italian dish made from wheat and water.

паста

pasta

пекарь | pékar'

Part of speech: noun

Gender: masculine

Baker, as in "The **baker** makes fresh bread every morning" (**Пекарь** печет свежий хлеб каждое утро.). It is a noun and is often used to describe a person who bakes and sells bread and other baked goods.

пекарь

baker

переводчик | perevódchik

Part of speech: noun

Gender: masculine

Translator, as in "The **translator** helped us understand the document" (**Переводчик** помог нам понять документ.). It is a noun and is often used to describe a person who translates spoken or written language from one language to another.

переводчик

translator

перед | péred

Part of speech: preposition

In front of, as in "The car is parked **in front of** the house" (Машина припаркована **перед** домом.). It is a preposition and is often used to indicate a position that is ahead of or facing something.

перед

in front of

перед тем как | péred tém kak

Part of speech: conjunction

Before, as in "Wash your hands **before** eating" (Вымойте руки **перед тем как** есть.). It is a conjunction used to introduce a clause that indicates an action occurring prior to another action.

перед тем как

before

перекрёсток | perekryóstok

Part of speech: noun

Gender: masculine

Intersection, as in "The traffic light at the **intersection** is red" (Светофор на **перекрёстке** красный.). It is a noun and is often used to describe a place where two or more roads cross each other.

перекрёсток

intersection

перец | pérets

Part of speech: noun

Gender: masculine

Pepper, as in "I added **pepper** to the soup" (Я добавил **перец** в суп.). It is a noun and can refer to both the spice made from ground peppercorns and the vegetable, such as bell pepper.

перец

pepper

печень | péchen'

Part of speech: noun

Gender: feminine

Liver, as in "The **liver i**s an essential organ for detoxification" (**Печень** — это важный орган для детоксикации.). It is a noun and refers to the organ in the body that processes nutrients and detoxifies substances.

печень

liver

пешеходный переход | peshekhódny perekhód

Part of speech: noun phrase

Gender: masculine

Crosswalk, as in "Please use the **crosswalk** to ensure your safety" (Пожалуйста, пользуйтесь **пешеходным переходом** для вашей безопасности.). It is an imperative sentence and is often used to instruct or request someone to cross the street at a designated pedestrian crossing.

пешеходный переход

crosswalk

пешком | peshkóm

Part of speech: adverb

On foot, as in "I go to work **on foot** every day" (Я хожу на работу **пешком** каждый день.).
It is an adverb and is often used to describe the action of walking rather than using a vehicle.

пешком

on foot

пиво | pívo

Part of speech: noun

Gender: neuter

Beer, as in "I enjoy a cold **beer** on a hot day" (Я наслаждаюсь холодным **пивом** в жаркий день.). It is a noun and is often used to refer to the alcoholic beverage made from fermented grains.

пиво

beer

писать | pisát' (Imperfective)

Perfective: написать | napisát'

Part of speech: verb
Verb group: -ать

To write, as in "I like **to write** letters" (Я люблю **писать** письма.).
It is a verb and is often used to describe the action of composing text.

писать

to write

пить | pit' (Imperfective)

Perfective: выпить | výpit'

Part of speech: verb
Verb group: -ить

To drink, as in "I like **to drink** water after exercising" (Я люблю **пить** воду после тренировки.). It is a verb and is often used to describe the action of consuming liquids.

пить

to drink

пицца | píttsa

Gender: feminine

Part of speech: noun

Pizza, as in "We ordered a **pizza** for dinner" (Мы заказали **пиццу** на ужин.).
It is a noun and is often used to refer to a popular Italian dish.

пицца

pizza

плавание | plávanie

Gender: neuter

Part of speech: noun

Swimming, as in "**Swimming** is a great way to stay fit" (**Плавание** — отличный способ поддерживать форму.). It is a noun and is often used to describe the activity of moving through water using one's body.

плавание

swimming

плавать | plávat' (Imperfective)

Perfective: поплавать | poplávat'

Part of speech: verb
Verb group: -ать

Swim, as in "I **swim** in the pool every morning" (Я **плаваю** в бассейне каждое утро.).
It is a verb and is used to describe the action of moving through water.

плавать

to swim

плакать | plákat' (Imperfective)

Perfective: заплакать | zaplákat'

Part of speech: verb
Verb group: -ать

Cry, as in "The child began **to cry** when he lost his toy" (Ребёнок начал **плакать**, когда
потерял свою игрушку.). It is a verb and is used to describe the action of shedding tears.

плакать

to cry

план города | plan góroda

Gender: masculine

Part of speech: noun

City map, as in "I need a **city map** to find the museum" (Мне нужен **план города**, чтобы
найти музей.). It is a noun and is often used to refer to a map that shows the layout of a city.

план города

city map

платить | platít (Imperfective)

Perfective: заплатить | zaplátit'

Part of speech: verb
Verb group: -ить

To pay, as in "I need **to pay** the bill" (Мне нужно **заплатить** по счету.). It is a verb and
is often used to describe the action of giving money in exchange for goods or services.

платить

to pay

плечо | plechó

Part of speech: noun

Gender: neuter

Shoulder, as in "He tapped me on the **shoulder**" (Он постучал меня по **плечу**.). It is a noun and is often used to refer to the part of the body where the arm is connected to the torso.

плечо

shoulder

плотник | plótnik

Part of speech: noun

Gender: masculine

Carpenter, as in "The **carpenter** built a beautiful table" (**Плотник** построил красивый стол.). It is a noun and is often used to refer to a person who works with wood to construct or repair building frameworks and structures.

плотник

carpenter

плохо | plókho

Part of speech: adverb

Badly, as in "He sings **badly**" (Он **плохо** поёт.). It is an adverb and is often used to describe the manner in which an action is performed, indicating a lack of quality or skill.

плохо

badly, poorly

плохой | plokhóy

Part of speech: adjective

Bad, as in "This is a **bad** idea" (Это **плохая** идея.). It is an adjective and is often used to describe something of poor quality or unfavorable nature.

плохой

bad

площадь | plóshchad'

Part of speech: noun

Gender: feminine

Square, as in "The main **square** of the city is very beautiful" (Главная **площадь** города очень красивая.). It refers to an open public space in a city or town.

площадь

square, area

пляж | plyazh

Part of speech: noun

Gender: masculine

Beach, as in "We spent the whole day at the **beach**" (Мы провели весь день на **пляже**.). It is a noun and is often used to refer to a sandy or pebbly shore by the ocean, sea, lake, or river.

пляж

beach

побеждать | pobezhdát' (Imperfective)

Part of speech: verb
Verb group: -ать

Perfective: победить | pobedít'

To win, as in "Our team always **wins**" (Наша команда всегда **побеждает**.).
It is a verb used to describe the act of achieving victory in a competition or conflict.

побеждать

to win

поблизости | poblízosti

Part of speech: adverb

Nearby, as in "There is a park **nearby**" (**Поблизости** есть парк.). It is an adverb used to indicate that something is located close to a particular place or person.

поблизости

nearby

повар | pо́var

Part of speech: noun

Gender: masculine

Chef, as in "The **chef** prepared a delicious meal" (**Повар** приготовил вкусное блюдо.).
It is a noun used to refer to a person who prepares and cooks food, especially as a profession.

повар

chef, cook

поворачивать | povoráchivat' (Imperfective)

Part of speech: verb
Verb group: -ать

Perfective: повернуть | povernút'

To turn, as in "**Turn** left at the next street" (**Поверните** налево на следующей
улице.). It is a verb used to describe the action of changing direction or orientation.

поворачивать

to turn

повышение | povyshénie

Part of speech: noun

Gender: neuter

Promotion, as in "She received a **promotion** at work" (Она получила **повышение** на
работе.). It is a noun and is often used to refer to the advancement in rank or position.

повышение

promotion

погода | pogóda

Part of speech: noun

Gender: feminine

Weather, as in "The **weather** is nice today" (Сегодня хорошая **погода**.). It is a noun
and is often used to describe the atmospheric conditions at a particular time and place.

погода

weather

пограничный контроль | pograníchny kontról

Part of speech: noun phrase

Gender: masculine

Border control, as in "We passed through **border control** quickly" (Мы быстро прошли **пограничный контроль**.). It is a noun phrase used to describe the measures and procedures used by a country to monitor and regulate its borders, typically involving the inspection of travelers and goods.

пограничный контроль

border control

подбородок | podboródok

Part of speech: noun

Gender: masculine

Chin, as in "He rested his **chin** on his hand" (Он оперся **подбородком** на руку.).
It is a noun used to describe the part of the face below the mouth and above the neck.

подбородок

chin

подработка | podrabótka

Part of speech: noun

Gender: feminine

Side job, as in "He took a **side job** to save money for a vacation" (Он устроился на **подработку**, чтобы накопить на отпуск.). It is a noun used to describe additional work taken on alongside one's main job, often to earn extra income.

подработка

side job

поезд | póyezd

Part of speech: noun

Gender: masculine

Train, as in "The **train** arrived at the station on time" (**Поезд** прибыл на станцию вовремя.).
It is a noun used to describe a mode of transportation consisting of a series of connected vehicles that run on a track and are used for transporting passengers or goods.

поезд

train

поездка | payézdka

Part of speech: noun

Gender: feminine

Trip, as in "We are planning a **trip** to the mountains" (Мы планируем **поездку** в горы.).
It is a noun used to describe an excursion or journey to a particular place, often for leisure or business purposes.

поездка

trip, journey

пожалуйста | pozhaluysta

Part of speech: particle

Please, as in "Could you pass the salt, **please**?" (Можете передать соль, **пожалуйста**?). It is a particle and is often used to make polite requests.

пожалуйста

please

позавчера | pozavcherá

Part of speech: adverb

Day before yesterday, as in "I met him the **day before yesterday**" (Я встретил его **позавчера**.).
It is an adverb and is often used to refer to the day that occurred two days prior to the current day.

позавчера

day before yesterday

позже | pózzhe

Part of speech: adverb

Later, as in "I will call you **later**" (Я позвоню тебе **позже**.). It is an adverb and is often used to indicate that something will happen after the present time or at a future time.

позже

later

пока | poká

Part of speech: Particle/Conjunction

Bye, as in "**Bye**, see you tomorrow!" (**Пока**, увидимся завтра!).
It is a particle and is often used as an informal farewell.

пока

bye

показывать | pokazývat' (Imperfective)

Part of speech: verb
Verb group: -ать

Perfective: показать | pokazát'

To show, as in "Can you **show** me how to do this?" (Можешь **показать** мне, как это сделать?). It is a verb and is often used to describe the act of demonstrating or displaying something to someone.

показывать

to show

покупать | pokupát' (Imperfective)

Part of speech: verb
Verb group: -ать

Perfective: купить | kupít'

To buy, as in "I want **to buy** a new book" (Я хочу **купить** новую книгу.). It is a verb and is often used to describe the act of acquiring something in exchange for money.

покупать

to buy

полдень | pólden'

Part of speech: noun

Gender: masculine

Noon, as in "Let's meet at **noon**" (Давай встретимся в **полдень**.).
It is a noun and is often used to refer to 12:00 PM, the middle of the day.

полдень

noon

полицейский | politseýskiy

Part of speech: noun

Gender: masculine

Police officer, as in "The **police officer** helped the lost child" (**Полицейский** помог потерявшемуся ребёнку.). It is a noun and is often used to refer to a member of the police force.

полицейский

police officer

полиция | polítsiya

Part of speech: noun

Gender: feminine

Police, as in "The **police** arrived quickly at the scene" (**Полиция** быстро прибыла на место происшествия.). It is a noun and is often used to refer to the organized civil force responsible for maintaining public order and safety.

полиция

police

полночь | pólnoch'

Part of speech: noun

Gender: feminine

Midnight, as in "The event starts at **midnight**" (Мероприятие начинается в **полночь**.). It is a noun and is often used to refer to 12:00 AM, the middle of the night.

полночь

midnight

полный рабочий день | pólnyy rabóchiy den'

Part of speech: noun phrase

Gender: masculine

Full-time, as in "She works **full-time** at the company" (Она работает **полный рабочий день** в компании.). It is a noun phrase and is often used to describe a work schedule that typically involves a standard number of hours, often around 40 hours per week.

полный рабочий день

full-time

ПОМНИТЬ | pómnit' (Imperfective)

Part of speech: verb
Verb group: -ить

Perfective: запомнить | zapómnit'

Remember, as in "I **remember** my childhood vividly" (Я **помню** своё детство ярко.). It is a verb and is often used to describe the act of recalling information or experiences from the past.

помнить

to remember

ПОМОГАТЬ | pomogát' (Imperfective)

Part of speech: verb
Verb group: -ать

Perfective: помочь | pomóch'

Help, as in "I **help** my friends with their homework" (Я **помогаю** своим друзьям с домашним заданием.). It is a verb and is often used to describe the act of providing assistance or support to someone.

помогать

to help

ПОМОЩЬ | pómoshch'

Part of speech: noun

Gender: feminine

Help, as in "She asked for **help** with the project" (Она попросила **помощь** с проектом.).
It is a noun and is often used to refer to the act of providing support or assistance to someone.

помощь

help, assistance

понедельник | ponedélnik

Part of speech: noun

Gender: masculine

Monday, as in "We have a meeting on **Monday**" (У нас встреча в **понедельник**.).
It is a noun and is often used to refer to the first day of the workweek in many cultures.

понедельник

Monday

понимать | ponimát' (Imperfective)

Perfective: понять | ponyát'

Part of speech: verb
Verb group: -ать

Understand, as in "I **understand** the lesson well" (Я хорошо **понимаю** урок.). It is a verb and is often used to describe the act of comprehending or grasping the meaning of something.

понимать

to understand

после полудня | pósle polúdnya

Part of speech: prepositional phrase

In the afternoon, as in "We will meet **in the afternoon**" (Мы встретимся **после полудня**.). This phrase is used to refer to the time period after noon and before evening.

после полудня

in the afternoon

после того как | pósle togo kak

Part of speech: conjunction

After, as in "We went for a walk **after** we finished our work" (Мы пошли на прогулку **после того как** закончили работу.). This conjunction is used to introduce a clause that describes an event occurring subsequent to another event.

после того как

after

послезавтра | bezháť

Part of speech: adverb

Day after tomorrow, as in "We will go to the beach the **day after tomorrow**" (Мы поедем на пляж **послезавтра**.). This adverb is used to refer to the day that comes two days after the current day.

послезавтра

day after tomorrow

потому что | potomú chto

Part of speech: conjunction

Because, as in "I stayed home **because** it was raining" (Я остался дома, **потому что** шёл дождь.). This conjunction is used to introduce a reason or explanation for something.

потому что

because

поход | pokhód

Part of speech: noun

Gender: masculine

Hike, as in "We went on a **hike** in the mountains" (Мы отправились в **поход** в горы.). It is a noun and is often used to describe a long walk, especially in the countryside or wilderness.

поход

hike

почему | pochemy

Part of speech: adverb

Why, as in "**Why** are you late?" (**Почему** ты опоздал?). It is an adverb and is often used to ask for the reason or explanation for something.

почему

why

почта | póchta

Part of speech: verb
Verb group: irregular

Gender: feminine

Post Office, as in "I need to go to the **post office** to send a package" (Мне нужно сходить на **почту**, чтобы отправить посылку.). It is a noun and is often used to describe the place where mail is sent and received.

почта

post office

почти | pochti

Part of speech: adverb

Almost, as in "I am **almost** finished with my work" (Я **почти** закончил свою работу.). It is an adverb and is often used to indicate that something is nearly, but not completely, done or true.

почти

almost

правильный | právil'nyy

Part of speech: adjective

Right, as in "He made the **right** decision" (Он принял **правильное** решение.).
It is an adjective and is often used to describe something that is morally good, justified, or acceptable.

правильный

right

праздник | prázdnik

Part of speech: noun

Gender: masculine

Holiday, as in "New Year's Day is a **holiday**" (Новый год — это **праздник**.). It is a noun and is often used to describe a day of festivity or recreation when no work is done.

праздник

holiday, celebration

предприятие| bezháť

Part of speech: verb
Verb group: irregular

Gender: neuter

Business, as in "The **business** has been operating for over ten years" (**Предприятие** работает уже более десяти лет.). It is a noun and is often used to describe a company or firm engaged in commercial, industrial, or professional activities.

предприятие

business

преподавать | prepodavát' (Imperfective)

Part of speech: verb
Verb group: -ать

Perfective: преподать | prepodát'

To teach, as in "She loves **to teach** mathematics" (Она любит **преподавать** математику.).
It is a verb and is often used to describe the act of imparting knowledge or instructing someone in a subject or skill.

преподавать

to teach

привет | privét

Part of speech: interjection

Hello, as in "**Hello**, how are you?" (**Привет**, как дела?).
It is an interjection and is often used as a casual greeting.

привет

hello

приключение | priklyuchéniye

Part of speech: noun

Gender: neuter

Adventure, as in "The book is about an exciting **adventure**." (Книга о захватывающем **приключении**.). It is a noun and is often used to describe an exciting or unusual experience.

приключение

adventure

приходить | prikhodít' (Imperfective)

Part of speech: verb
Verb group: -ить

Perfective: прийти | priytí

Come, as in "She **comes** to the office every morning." (Она **приходит** в офис каждое утро.). It is a verb and is used to describe the action of arriving at a place.

приходить

to come

пробовать | próbovat' (Imperfective)

Perfective: попробовать | popróbovat'

Part of speech: verb
Verb group: -овать
special subgroup of the -ать verb group

Try, as in "I **try** new foods whenever I travel." (Я **пробую** новую еду, когда путешествую.).
It is a verb and is used to describe the action of making an attempt or effort to do something.

пробовать

to try

прогноз погоды | prognóz pogódy

Gender: masculine

Part of speech: noun phrase

Weather forecast, as in "The **weather forecast** predicts rain tomorrow." (**Прогноз погоды** предсказывает дождь завтра.). It is a noun phrase and is often used to describe a report on expected weather conditions.

прогноз погоды

weather forecast

продавать | prodavát' (Imperfective)

Perfective: продать | prodát'

Part of speech: verb
Verb group: -ать

Sell, as in "They **sell** fresh vegetables at the market." (Они **продают** свежие овощи на рынке.).
It is a verb and is used to describe the action of exchanging goods or services for money.

продавать

to sell

продавец | prodavéts

Gender: masculine

Part of speech: noun

Salesperson, as in "The **salesperson** was very friendly and helpful." (**Продавец** был очень дружелюбным и отзывчивым.). It is a noun and is often used to describe a person who sells goods or services, typically in a retail environment.

продавец

salesperson

проездной билет | proyezdnóy bilét

Part of speech: noun phrase

Gender: masculine

Travel ticket, as in "I bought a **travel ticket** for the subway." (Я купил **проездной билет** для метро.). It is a noun phrase used to describe a ticket that allows for travel on public transportation.

проездной билет

travel ticket

простой | prostóy

Part of speech: adjective

Easy, as in "The task was **easy** to complete." (Задача была **простой** для выполнения.). It is an adjective used to describe something that requires little effort or is not difficult to accomplish.

простой

easy

профессия | professiya

Part of speech: noun

Gender: feminine

Profession, as in "She chose medicine as her **profession**." (Она выбрала медицину в качестве своей **профессии**.). It is a noun used to describe a type of job that requires special education, training, or skill.

профессия

profession

прохладно | prokhládno

Part of speech: adverb

Cool, as in "It is **cool** outside today." (Сегодня на улице **прохладно**.). It is an adverb used to describe a moderately low temperature, often pleasantly so.

прохладно

cool

прощать | proshchát' (Imperfective)

Perfective: простить | prostít'

Part of speech: verb
Verb group: -ать

Forgive, as in "She decided **to forgive** him for his mistake" (Она решила **простить** его за ошибку.). It is a verb and is used to describe the act of forgiving someone.

прощать

to forgive

прыгать | prýgat' (Imperfective)

Perfective: прыгнуть | prýgnut'

Part of speech: verb
Verb group: -ать

Jump, as in "The children love **to jump** on the trampoline" (Дети любят **прыгать** на батуте.). It is a verb and is used to describe the action of jumping.

прыгать

to jump

прямо | pryámo

Part of speech: adverb

Straight ahead, as in "Go **straight ahead** and you will see the museum" (Идите **прямо**, и вы увидите музей.). It is an adverb and is often used to describe moving in a straight direction.

прямо

straight ahead

птица | ptítsa

Gender: feminine

Part of speech: noun

Bird, as in "The **bird** is singing in the tree" (**Птица** поёт на дереве.).
It is a noun and is often used to refer to a feathered animal that can fly.

птица

bird

пункт назначения | punkt naznachéniya

Part of speech: noun phrase

Gender: masculine

Destination, as in "We have finally reached our **destination**" (Мы наконец-то достигли нашего **пункта назначения**.). It is a noun phrase used to refer to the place to which someone or something is going or being sent.

пункт назначения

destination

пунктуальный | punktuál'nyy

Part of speech: adjective

Punctual, as in "He is always **punctual** for meetings" (Он всегда **пунктуален** на встречах.). It is an adjective used to describe someone who arrives or does something at the expected or planned time.

пунктуальный

punctual

путеводитель | putevodítel'

Part of speech: noun

Gender: masculine

Guidebook, as in "I bought a **guidebook** for my trip to Paris" (Я купил **путеводитель** для моей поездки в Париж.). It is a noun used to refer to a book of information about a place, designed for the use of visitors or tourists.

путеводитель

guidebook

путешествовать | puteshéstvovat' (Imperfective)

Part of speech: verb
Verb group: -овать
special subgroup of the -ать verb group

Perfective: попутешествовать | poputeshéstvovat'

Travel, as in "I love **to travel** to new countries" (Я люблю **путешествовать** в новые страны.). It is a verb and is often used to describe the act of going from one place to another for leisure or exploration.

путешествовать

to travel

пятнадцать | pyatnádtsat'

Part of speech: numeral

Fifteen, as in "She has **fifteen** books on her shelf" (У неё на полке **пятнадцать** книг.). It is a numeral and is often used to denote the quantity of fifteen.

пятнадцать

fifteen

пятница | pyátnitsa

Part of speech: noun

Gender: feminine

Friday, as in "We will meet on **Friday**" (Мы встретимся в **пятницу**.).
It is a noun and is often used to refer to the fifth day of the week.

пятница

Friday

пять | pyat'

Part of speech: numeral

Five, as in "There are **five** apples on the table" (На столе **пять** яблок.).
It is a numeral and is often used to denote the quantity of five.

пять

five

пятьдесят | pyat'desyát

Part of speech: numeral

Fifty, as in "He ran **fifty** kilometers last week" (Он пробежал **пятьдесят** километров на прошлой неделе.). It is a numeral and is often used to denote the quantity of fifty.

пятьдесят

fifty

пятьсот | pyatsót

Part of speech: numeral

Five hundred, as in "The book costs **five hundred** rubles" (Книга стоит **пятьсот** рублей.). It is a numeral and is often used to denote the quantity of five hundred.

пятьсот

five hundred

работа | rabóta

Part of speech: noun

Gender: feminine

Work, as in "She enjoys her **work** at the company" (Она наслаждается своей **работой** в компании.). It is a noun and is often used to refer to tasks or duties performed as part of employment or occupation.

работа

work, job

работать | rabótat' (Imperfective)

Part of speech: verb
Verb group: -ать

Perfective: поработать | porabótat'

To work, as in "I need **to work** on this project today" (Мне нужно **работать** над этим проектом сегодня.). It is a verb and is often used to describe the act of performing tasks or duties, typically as part of employment.

работать

to work

работник | rabótnik

Part of speech: noun

Gender: masculine

Employee, as in "The **employee** received a promotion for his hard work" (**Работник** получил повышение за свою усердную работу.). It is a noun and is often used to refer to a person who works for a company or organization.

работник

employee, worker

работодатель | rabotodátel'

Part of speech: noun

Gender: masculine

Employer, as in "The **employer** offered new benefits to all employees" (**Работодатель** предложил новые льготы всем сотрудникам.). It is a noun and is often used to refer to a person or organization that hires and pays employees for their work.

работодатель

employer

рабочее место | rabóchee mésto

Part of Speech: noun phrase

Gender: neuter

Workplace, as in "She keeps her workplace organized and tidy" (Она держит своё рабочее место в порядке и чистоте.). It is a noun phrase and is often used to refer to the physical location where someone performs their job duties.

рабочее место

workplace

разрушать | razrushát' (Imperfective)

Part of speech: verb

Verb group: -ать

Perfective: разрушить | razrúshit'

Destroy, as in "The storm can **destroy** buildings" (Шторм может **разрушать** здания.). It is a verb and is often used to describe the act of causing something to be damaged or demolished.

разрушать

to destroy

раньше | rán'she

Part of speech: adverb

Earlier, as in "I used to wake up **earlier**" (Я раньше вставал **раньше**.). It is an adverb and is often used to indicate a time prior to the present or a specified time.

раньше

earlier, before

рассвет | rassvét

Part of speech: noun

Gender: masculine

Dawn, as in "We decided to start our journey at **dawn**" (Мы решили начать наше путешествие на **рассвете**.). It is a noun and is often used to describe the time of day when light first appears in the sky before sunrise.

рассвет

dawn

ребёнок | rebёnok

Part of speech: noun

Gender: masculine

Child, as in "The **child** is playing in the park" (**Ребёнок** играет в парке.).
It is a noun and is often used to refer to a young human being.

ребёнок

child

редко | rédko

Part of speech: adjective

Rarely, as in "She **rarely** goes to the cinema" (Она **редко** ходит в кино.).
It is an adverb and is often used to describe something that does not happen often.

редко

rarely

резюме | rezyumé

Part of speech: noun

Gender: neuter

Résumé, as in "He updated his **résumé** before applying for the job" (Он обновил своё **резюме** перед подачей на работу.). It is a noun and is often used to refer to a document summarizing a person's education, qualifications, and previous experience.

резюме

résumé

ремесленник | reméslennik

Part of speech: noun

Gender: masculine

Craftsman, as in "The **craftsman** created beautiful wooden furniture" (**Ремесленник** создал красивую деревянную мебель.). It is a noun and is often used to refer to a person skilled in a particular craft or trade.

ремесленник

craftsman, artisan

ремонтировать | remontírovat' (Imperfective)

Part of speech: verb
Verb group: -овать
special subgroup of the -ать verb group

Perfective: отремонтировать | otremontírovat'

To repair, as in "He needs **to repair** the car" (Ему нужно **ремонтировать** машину.). It is a verb and is often used to describe the act of fixing or restoring something to a good condition.

ремонтировать

to repair

ресторан | restorán

Part of speech: noun

Gender: masculine

Restaurant, as in "We had dinner at a nice **restaurant**" (Мы поужинали в хорошем **ресторане**.). It is a noun and is often used to refer to a place where meals are prepared and served to customers.

ресторан

restaurant

рис | ris

Part of speech: noun

Gender: masculine

Rice, as in "She cooked **rice** for dinner" (Она приготовила **рис** на ужин.). It is a noun and is often used to refer to the starchy grain used as a staple food in many cultures.

рис

rice

рисовать | risovát' (Imperfective)

Perfective: нарисоват | narisovát'

Part of speech: verb
Verb group: -овать
special subgroup of the -ать verb group

To draw, as in "She likes **to draw** animals" (Она любит **рисовать** животных.). It is a verb and is often used to describe the act of creating images on a surface, typically paper, using a pencil, pen, or brush.

рисовать

to draw

рот | rot

Gender: masculine

Part of speech: noun

Mouth, as in "He opened his **mouth** to speak" (Он открыл **рот**, чтобы заговорить.). It is a noun and is often used to refer to the opening in the face used for eating, speaking, and breathing.

рот

mouth

рука | ruká

Gender: feminine

Part of speech: noun

Arm, as in "He wore a watch on his left **arm**" (Он носил часы на левой **руке**.). It is a noun and is often used to refer to the upper limb of the human body, extending from the shoulder to the hand.

рука

arm

рыба | ryba

Gender: feminine

Part of speech: noun

Fish, as in "She caught a big **fish** in the lake" (Она поймала большую **рыбу** в озере.). It is a noun and is often used to refer to aquatic animals that are typically covered with scales and equipped with fins.

рыба

fish

рынок | rynok

Part of speech: noun

Gender: masculine

Market, as in "They went to the **market** to buy fresh vegetables" (Они пошли на **рынок**, чтобы купить свежие овощи.). It is a noun and is often used to refer to a place where people buy and sell goods, typically in an open-air setting.

рынок

market

рюкзак | ryukzák

Part of speech: noun

Gender: masculine

Backpack, as in "She packed her books into the **backpack**" (Она сложила книги в **рюкзак**.). It is a noun and is often used to refer to a bag with shoulder straps that allow it to be carried on one's back, typically used by students or travelers.

рюкзак

backpack

рядом | ryádom

Part of speech: adverb

Next to, as in "The library is **next to** the school" (Библиотека находится **рядом** со школой.). It is an adverb and is often used to describe proximity or closeness in location.

рядом

next to, near

садовник | sadóvnik

Part of speech: noun

Gender: masculine

Gardener, as in "The **gardener** planted new flowers in the garden" (**Садовник** посадил новые цветы в саду.). It is a noun and is often used to refer to a person who tends and cultivates a garden as a pastime or profession.

садовник

gardener

салат | salát

Part of speech: noun

Gender: masculine

Salad, as in "She prepared a fresh **salad** for lunch" (Она приготовила свежий **салат** на обед.). It is a noun and is often used to refer to a dish consisting of mixed pieces of food, typically with at least one raw ingredient, such as vegetables or fruits.

салат

salad

салфетка | salfétka

Part of speech: noun

Gender: feminine

Napkin, as in "He placed a **napkin** on his lap before eating" (Он положил **салфетку** на колени перед едой.). It is a noun and is often used to refer to a small piece of cloth or paper used at a meal to wipe the fingers or lips and to protect garments.

салфетка

napkin

самолёт | samolyót

Part of speech: noun

Gender: masculine

Airplane, as in "The **airplane** took off smoothly from the runway" (**Самолёт** плавно взлетел с взлётной полосы.). It is a noun and is often used to refer to a powered flying vehicle with fixed wings and a weight greater than that of the air it displaces.

самолёт

airplane

Санкт-Петербург | Sankt-Peterbúrg

Part of speech: noun

Saint Petersburg, as in "I visited **Saint Petersburg** last summer" (Я посетил **Санкт-Петербург** прошлым летом.). It is a proper noun and is often used to refer to the major Russian city known for its cultural and historical significance.

Санкт-Петербург

Saint Petersburg

сантехник | santékhnik

Part of speech: noun

Gender: masculine

Plumber, as in "The **plumber** fixed the leaking pipe" (**Сантехник** починил протекающую трубу.). It is a noun and is often used to refer to a person whose job is to install and repair water pipes and fixtures.

сантехник

plumber

сахар | sáhar

Part of speech: noun

Gender: masculine

Sugar, as in "I need some **sugar** for my coffee" (Мне нужен **сахар** для моего кофе.). It is a noun and is often used to refer to a sweet substance obtained from various plants, used to sweeten food and drinks.

сахар

sugar

сверхурочная работа | sverkhurochnaya rabóta

Part of speech: noun phrase

Gender: feminine

Overtime work, as in "She often does **overtime work** to meet deadlines" (Она часто выполняет **сверхурочную работу,** чтобы уложиться в сроки.). It is a noun phrase and is often used to refer to work done beyond regular working hours.

сверхурочная работа

overtime work

светофор | svetofór

Part of speech: noun

Gender: masculine

Traffic light, as in "The **traffic light** turned green" (**Светофор** загорелся зелёным.). It is a noun and is often used to refer to a signaling device positioned at road intersections to control the flow of traffic.

светофор

traffic light

свинина | svinína

Part of speech: noun

Gender: feminine

Pork, as in "She cooked **pork** for dinner" (Она приготовила **свинину** на ужин.).
It is a noun and is often used to refer to the meat from a pig, commonly used in cooking.

свинина

pork

свободный | svobódnyy

Part of speech: adjective

Free, as in "I am **free** this evening" (Я **свободен** этим вечером.). It is an adjective and is
often used to describe someone or something that is not occupied, restricted, or in use.

свободный

free

сегодня | segódnya

Part of speech: adverb

Today, as in "**Today** is a beautiful day" (**Сегодня** прекрасный день.).
It is an adverb and is used to refer to the current day.

сегодня

today

сейчас | seychás

Part of speech: adverb

Now, as in "I am busy right **now**" (Я **сейчас** занят.). It is an adverb used
to indicate the present moment or a very short time before or after it.

сейчас

now

секретарь | sekretár'

Part of speech: noun

Gender: masculine

Secretary, as in "The **secretary** organized the meeting" (**Секретарь** организовал встречу.). It is a noun used to refer to a person employed to handle correspondence, keep records, and do other administrative tasks.

секретарь

secretary

секунда | sekúnda

Part of speech: noun

Gender: feminine

Second, as in "Wait a **second**" (Подожди **секунду**.). It is a noun used to refer to a unit of time equal to one sixtieth of a minute.

секунда

second

семнадцать | semnádtsat'

Part of speech: numeral

Seventeen, as in "She is **seventeen** years old" (Ей **семнадцать** лет.). It is a numeral and is often used to denote the quantity or position in a sequence.

семнадцать

seventeen

семь | syém'

Part of speech: numeral

Seven, as in "There are **seven** days in a week" (В неделе **семь** дней.). It is a numeral and is often used to indicate quantity or count.

семь

seven

семьдесят | syém'desyat

Part of speech: numeral

Seventy, as in "The book has **seventy** pages" (В книге **семьдесят** страниц.).
It is a numeral and is often used to indicate quantity or count.

семьдесят

seventy

семьсот | syém'sot

Part of speech: numeral

Seven hundred, as in "The stadium can hold **seven hundred** people" (Стадион вмещает **семьсот** человек.). It is a numeral and is often used to indicate quantity or count.

семьсот

seven hundred

семья | sem'yá

Part of speech: noun

Gender: feminine

Family, as in "My **family** is very supportive" (Моя **семья** очень поддерживает меня.).
It is a noun and is often used to refer to a group of related individuals living together.

семья

family

сердце | sérdtse

Part of speech: noun

Gender: neuter

Heart, as in "His **heart** was beating fast" (Его **сердце** быстро билось.). It is a noun and is often used to refer to the organ that pumps blood through the body or metaphorically to describe emotions.

сердце

heart

сёрфинг | syórfing

Part of speech: noun

Gender: masculine

Surfing, as in "**Surfing** is a popular sport in Hawaii" (**Сёрфинг** — популярный спорт на Гавайях.). It is a noun and is often used to describe the activity of riding waves on a surfboard.

сёрфинг

surfing

сестра | sestrá

Part of speech: noun

Gender: feminine

Sister, as in "My **sister** is a doctor" (Моя **сестра** — врач.).
It is a noun and is used to refer to a female sibling.

сестра

sister

сидеть | sidét' (Imperfective)

Part of speech: verb
Verb group: -еть

Perfective: сесть | sest'

To sit, as in "He likes **to sit** by the window" (Он любит **сидеть** у окна.).
It is a verb used to describe the action of being seated.

сидеть

to sit

сказать | skazát' (Perfective)

Part of speech: verb
Verb group: irregular

Imperfective: говорить | govarít'

Say, as in "She wants **to say** something important" (Она хочет **сказать** что-то важное.). It is a verb and is often used to express speaking or telling something.

сказать

to say, to tell

скалолазание | skalolázaniye

Part of speech: noun

Gender: neuter

Rock climbing, as in "**Rock climbing** is a challenging sport" (**Скалолазание** — это сложный спорт.). It is a noun and is often used to describe the activity of climbing rock formations.

скалолазание

rock climbing

сколько | skól'ko

Part of speech: pronoun

How many, as in "**How many** apples do you have?" (**Сколько** у тебя яблок?).
It is a pronoun and is often used to ask about the quantity or amount of something.

сколько

how much, how many

скоро | skóro

Part of speech: adverb

Soon, as in "I will be home **soon**" (Я **скоро** буду дома.). It is an adverb and is used to indicate that something will happen in the near future.

скоро

soon

скучный | skúčnyy

Part of speech: adjective

Boring, as in "The lecture was **boring**" (Лекция была **скучной**.). It is an adjective used to describe something that lacks interest or excitement.

скучный

boring, dull

сладкий | sládkiy

Part of speech: adjective

Sweet, as in "This cake is very **sweet**" (Этот торт очень **сладкий**.). It is an adjective used to describe something that has a sugary taste or is pleasant and agreeable.

сладкий

sweet

сливочное масло | slívochnoye máslo

Part of speech: noun phrase

Gender: neuter

Butter, as in "I need to buy **butter** for the recipe" (Мне нужно купить **сливочное масло** для рецепта.). It is a noun phrase used to refer to the dairy product made from churning cream.

сливочное масло

butter

случайно | slucháyno

Part of speech: adverb

By chance, as in "**By chance**, I met an old friend at the café yesterday" (**Случайно** я встретил старого друга в кафе вчера.). It is an adverb and is often used to describe something that happens without intention or unexpectedly.

случайно

by chance, accidentally

слышать | slýshat' (Imperfective)

Part of speech: verb
Verb group: -ать

Perfective: услышать | uslýshat'

To hear, as in "I can **hear** the music from my room" (Я могу **слышать** музыку из своей комнаты.). It is a verb and is often used to describe the ability to perceive sounds.

слышать

to hear

смеяться | smeyát'sya (Imperfective)

Perfective: засмеяться | zasmeját'sya

Part of speech: verb
Verb group: -яться
special and rare verb group

To laugh, as in "They always **laugh** at his jokes" (Они всегда **смеются** над его шутками.).
It is a verb and is often used to describe the action of expressing amusement or joy.

смеяться

to laugh

снаружи | snarúzhi

Part of speech: adverb

Outside, as in "The cat is **outside** the house" (Кошка **снаружи** дома.). It is an adverb
and is often used to describe a location that is not inside a building or structure.

снаружи

outside

снег | sneg

Gender: masculine

Part of speech: noun

Snow, as in "The **snow** is falling softly" (**Снег** падает мягко.). It is a noun and is
often used to describe frozen precipitation that falls from the sky in cold weather.

снег

snow

сноубординг | sneg

Gender: masculine

Part of speech: noun

Snowboarding, as in "**Snowboarding** is a popular winter sport" (**Сноубординг** — популярный
зимний спорт.). It is a noun and refers to the activity or sport of riding a snowboard down a
snow-covered slope.

сноубординг

snowboarding

собака | sobáka

Part of speech: noun

Gender: feminine

Dog, as in "The **dog** is playing in the yard" (**Собака** играет во дворе.). It is a noun and refers to a domesticated carnivorous mammal that typically has a long snout and an acute sense of smell.

собака

dog

собеседование | sobesédovaniye

Part of speech: noun

Gender: neuter

Job Interview, as in "She received an invitation for a **job interview** at a large company" (Она получила приглашение на **собеседование** в крупную компанию.). It is a noun and refers to the process where a candidate is evaluated for a position in the context of employment.

собеседование

job interview

современный | sovreménnyy

Part of speech: adjective

Modern, as in "The building has a **modern** design" (Здание имеет **современный** дизайн.). It is an adjective used to describe something that is characteristic of the present or recent times, often in contrast with the past.

современный

modern

сок | sok

Part of speech: noun

Gender: masculine

Juice, as in "He drank a glass of orange **juice**" (Он выпил стакан апельсинового **сока**.). It is a noun referring to the liquid that is naturally contained in fruit and vegetables.

сок

juice

соленый | solyónyy

Part of speech: adjective

Salty, as in "The soup is too **salty**" (Суп слишком **солёный**.). It is an adjective used to describe something that contains or is seasoned with salt.

соленый

salty

солнечно | sólnechno

Part of speech: adverb

Sunny, as in "It is **sunny** outside today" (Сегодня на улице **солнечно**.).
It is an adverb used to describe weather conditions characterized by bright sunlight.

солнечно

sunny

солнечные очки | sólnechnyye ochkí

Part of speech: noun phrase

Gender: plural

Sunglasses, as in "I always wear **sunglasses** on sunny days" (Я всегда ношу **солнечные очки** в солнечные дни.). It is a noun phrase referring to glasses tinted to protect the eyes from sunlight.

солнечные очки

sunglasses

солнце | sólntse

Part of speech: noun

Gender: neuter

Sun, as in "The **sun** is shining brightly" (**Солнце** ярко светит.). It is a noun referring to the star at the center of our solar system, which provides light and heat to the Earth.

солнце

sun

соломинка| solomínka

Part of speech: noun

Gender: feminine

Straw, as in "She drank her juice through a **straw**" (Она пила сок через **соломинку**.).
It is a noun referring to a thin tube used for sucking liquid into the mouth.

соломинка

straw

соль | sol'

Part of speech: noun

Gender: feminine

Salt, as in "Please pass the **salt**" (Пожалуйста, передай **соль**.). It is a noun
referring to a white crystalline substance used for seasoning and preserving food.

соль

salt

сорок| sórok

Part of speech: numeral

Forty, as in "He is **forty** years old" (Ему **сорок** лет.).
It is a numeral used to represent the number 40.

сорок

forty

сотрудник | sotrúdnik

Part of speech: noun

Gender: masculine

Employee, as in "The **employee** is working on the project" (**Сотрудник** работает над проектом.).
It is a noun and is often used to refer to a person who works for a company or organization.

сотрудник

employee

спасибо | spasíbo

Part of speech: interjection

Thank you, as in "**Thank you** for your help" (**Спасибо** за вашу помощь.).
It is an interjection and is often used to express gratitude.

спасибо

thank you

спать | spat' (Imperfective)

Part of speech: verb
Verb group: -ать

Perfective: поспать | pospat'

Sleep, as in "I like **to sleep** early" (Я люблю **спать** рано.). It is a
verb and is used to describe the act of resting with eyes closed.

спать

to sleep

спина | spiná

Part of speech: noun

Gender: feminine

Back, as in "My **back** hurts after lifting heavy boxes" (У меня болит **спина** после поднятия
тяжёлых коробок.). It is a noun and is often used to refer to the rear part of the human body.

спина

back

спрашивать | spráshivat' (Imperfective)

Part of speech: verb
Verb group: -ать

Perfective: спросить | sprosít'

Ask, as in "I often **ask** questions in class" (Я часто **спрашиваю** вопросы в классе.).
It is a verb and is used to describe the act of inquiring or seeking information.

спрашивать

to ask

сразу | srázu

Part of speech: adverb

Immediately, as in "She answered **immediately** after the question was asked" (Она ответила **сразу** после того, как был задан вопрос.). It is an adverb and is often used to describe doing something without delay.

сразу

immediately, soon

среда | sredá

Part of speech: noun

Gender: feminine

Wednesday, as in "We have a meeting every **Wednesday**" (У нас собрание каждую **среду**.). It is a noun and is often used to refer to the third day of the week.

среда

Wednesday

стакан | stakán

Part of speech: noun

Gender: masculine

Glass, as in "I poured water into the **glass**" (Я налил воду в **стакан**.).
It is a noun and is often used to refer to a container used for drinking liquids.

стакан

glass

старомодный | staromódnyy

Part of speech: adjective

Old-fashioned, as in "He wore an **old-fashioned** suit to the party" (Он надел **старомодный** костюм на вечеринку.). It is an adjective used to describe something that is no longer in style or is characteristic of an earlier time.

старомодный

old-fashioned

старый | stáryy

Old, as in "He lives in an **old** house" (Он живёт в **старом** доме.). It is an adjective used to describe something that has existed for a long time or is not new.

старый

old

сто | sto

One hundred, as in "There are **one hundred** students in the school" (В школе **сто** учеников.). It is a numeral used to represent the quantity of 100.

сто

one hundred

сто тысяч | stáryy

One hundred thousand, as in "The city has a population of **one hundred thousand** people" (В городе население **сто тысяч** человек.). It is a numeral phrase used to represent the quantity of 100,000.

сто тысяч

one hundred thousand

стоить | stóit (Imperfective)

Cost, as in "How much does this book **cost**?" (Сколько **стоит** эта книга?). It is a verb and is often used to inquire about the price of something. **стоить** in the sense of "to cost" typically describes a state or quality, and such verbs often have no perfective equivalent, as is the case here.

стоить

to cost

стол | stol

Part of speech: noun

Gender: masculine

Table, as in "The book is on the **table**" (Книга на **столе**.). It is a noun and is often used to refer to a piece of furniture with a flat top and one or more legs, used for eating, writing, or working.

стол

table

столица | stolítsa

Part of speech: noun

Gender: feminine

Capital, as in "Moscow is the **capital** of Russia" (Москва — **столица** России.). It is a noun and is often used to refer to the city that serves as the seat of government and administrative center of a country or region.

столица

capital (city)

стоять | stoyát' (Imperfective)

Part of speech: verb
Verb group: irregular

Perfective: постоять | postoyát'

Stand, as in "He **stands** by the window" (Он **стоит** у окна.). It is a verb and is often used to describe the action of being in an upright position on one's feet.

стоять

to stand

страна | straná

Part of speech: noun

Gender: feminine

Country, as in "France is a beautiful **country**" (Франция — красивая **страна**.). It is a noun and is often used to refer to a nation with its own government, occupying a particular territory.

страна

country

страховка | strakhovka

Part of speech: noun

Gender: feminine

Insurance, as in "I need health **insurance**" (Мне нужна медицинская **страховка**.). It is a noun and is often used to refer to a contract in which an individual or entity receives financial protection or reimbursement against losses from an insurance company.

страховка

insurance

строитель | stroítel'

Part of speech: noun

Gender: masculine

Builder, as in "He works as a **builder**" (Он работает **строителем**.). It is a noun and is often used to refer to a person who constructs buildings or other structures.

строитель

builder

строить | stróit' (Imperfective)

Part of speech: verb
Verb group: -ить

Perfective: построить | postróit'

Build, as in "They are **building** a new house" (Они **строят** новый дом.). It is a verb and is often used to describe the action of constructing something, such as a building or structure.

строить

to build

стул | stul

Part of speech: noun

Gender: masculine

Chair, as in "The **chair** is in the kitchen" (**Стул** находится на кухне.). It is a noun and is used to refer to a piece of furniture designed for sitting, typically having four legs and a backrest.

стул

chair

ступня | stupnyá

Part of speech: noun

Gender: feminine

Foot, as in "My **foot** hurts" (У меня болит **ступня**.). It is a noun and is used to refer to the lower extremity of the leg below the ankle, on which a person stands or walks.

ступня

foot

суббота | subbóta

Part of speech: noun

Gender: feminine

Saturday, as in "We will meet on **Saturday**" (Мы встретимся в **субботу**.). It is a noun and refers to the day of the week following Friday and preceding Sunday.

суббота

Saturday

сувенир | suvenir

Part of speech: noun

Gender: masculine

Souvenir, as in "I bought a **souvenir** from my trip" (Я купил **сувенир** из поездки.). It is a noun and refers to an object kept as a reminder of a place, person, or event, often purchased by travelers.

сувенир

souvenir

суп | sup

Part of speech: noun

Gender: masculine

Soup, as in "The **soup** is delicious" (**Суп** вкусный.). It is a noun and refers to a liquid dish, typically made by boiling meat, fish, or vegetables in stock or water.

суп

soup

супермаркет | supermarket

Part of speech: noun

Gender: masculine

Supermarket, as in "I am going to the **supermarket**" (Я иду в **супермаркет**.).
It is a noun and refers to a large self-service store selling foods and household goods.

супермаркет

supermarket

сухо | sukho

Part of speech: adverb

Dryly, as in "He answered **dryly**" (Он ответил **сухо**.). It is an adverb used to describe the manner
of speaking or acting in a way that lacks warmth or emotion, often straightforward or blunt.

сухо

dryly

счастливый | schastlivyy

Part of speech: adjective

Happy, as in "She is **happy**" (Она **счастливая**.). It is an adjective
used to describe a state of joy, contentment, or satisfaction.

счастливый

happy

счет | schet

Part of speech: noun

Gender: masculine

Bill, as in "Could you bring the **bill**, please?" (Можете принести **счет**, пожалуйста?). It is a
noun and is often used in the context of paying for goods or services at a restaurant or store.

счет

bill

сын | syn

Part of speech: noun

Gender: masculine

Son, as in "My **son** is five years old" (Моему **сыну** пять лет.). It is a noun and is used to refer to a male child in relation to his parents.

сын

son

сыр | syr

Part of speech: noun

Gender: masculine

Cheese, as in "I like **cheese** on my sandwich" (Я люблю **сыр** в своем бутерброде.). It is a noun and is often used to refer to a dairy product made from curdled or cultured milk, commonly used in cooking and as a topping.

сыр

cheese

такси | taksi

Part of speech: noun

Gender: neuter

Taxi, as in "I will call a **taxi** to get to the airport" (Я вызову **такси**, чтобы добраться до аэропорта.). It is a noun and is often used to refer to a car licensed to transport passengers in return for payment of a fare.

такси

taxi

там | tam

Part of speech: adverb

There, as in "The book is over **there** on the table" (Книга **там**, на столе.). It is an adverb and is often used to indicate a location or place that is distant from the speaker.

там

there

танцевать | tantsevat' (Imperfective)

Part of speech: verb
Verb group: -ать

Perfective: потанцевать | potantseváť

To dance, as in "I love to dance at parties" (Я люблю танцевать на вечеринках.).
It is a verb and is used to describe the action of moving rhythmically to music.

танцевать

to dance

тарелка | tarélka

Part of speech: noun

Gender: feminine

Plate, as in "The soup is served on a **plate**" (Суп подается на **тарелке**.). It is a
noun and is often used to refer to a flat dish from which food is eaten or served.

тарелка

plate

таять | táyat' (Imperfective)

Part of speech: verb
Verb group: -ять
special and rare verb group

Perfective: растаять | rastáyat'

To melt, as in "The snow begins **to melt** in the spring" (Снег начинает **таять** весной.).
It is a verb used to describe the process of a solid becoming liquid due to heat.

таять

to melt, to thaw

твёрдый | tvyórdyi

Part of speech: adjective

Hard, as in "The table is made of **hard** wood" (Стол сделан из **твёрдого** дерева.).
It is an adjective used to describe something that is firm and resistant to pressure.

твёрдый

hard, solid

театр | teátr

Part of speech: noun

Gender: masculine

Theater, as in "We went to the **theater** to watch a play" (Мы пошли в **театр** смотреть спектакль.). It is a noun used to describe a building or venue where performances, such as plays and concerts, are presented.

театр

theater

тело | télo

Part of speech: noun

Gender: neuter

Body, as in "The human **body** is complex" (Человеческое **тело** сложно.).
It is a noun used to refer to the physical structure of a person or an organism.

тело

body

температура | temperatúra

Part of speech: noun

Gender: feminine

Temperature, as in "The **temperature** outside is very low today" (**Температура** на улице сегодня очень низкая.). It is a noun used to describe the degree of heat present in a substance or object, often measured in degrees Celsius or Fahrenheit.

температура

temperature

теннис | ténnis

Part of speech: noun

Gender: masculine

Tennis, as in "She plays **tennis** every weekend" (Она играет в **теннис** каждые выходные.).
It is a noun used to describe a sport in which two or four players strike a ball with rackets over a net stretched across a court.

теннис

tennis

теплый | tyóplyi

Part of speech: adjective

Warm, as in "The weather is **warm** today" (Сегодня **тёплая** погода.). It is an adjective used to describe a moderate degree of heat, often associated with comfort.

теплый

warm

терять | teryát (Imperfective)

Part of speech: verb
Verb group: -ять
special and rare verb group

Perfective: потерять | poteryát

To lose, as in "I often **lose** my keys" (Я часто **теряю** ключи.). It is a verb used to describe the act of misplacing or being unable to find something.

терять

to lose

тихий | tíkhiy

Part of speech: adjective

Quiet, as in "The library is a **quiet** place" (Библиотека — **тихое** место.).
It is an adjective used to describe a low level of noise or a peaceful environment.

тихий

quiet, silent

толкать | tolkát (Imperfective)

Part of speech: verb
Verb group: -ать

Perfective: толкнуть | tolknút'

To push, as in "He had **to push** the door to open it" (Ему пришлось **толкать** дверь, чтобы открыть её.). It is a verb used to describe the action of applying force to move something away or forward.

толкать

to push

толстый | tólsity

Part of speech: adjective

Thick, as in "The book is very **thick**" (Книга очень **толстая**.). It is an adjective used to describe something that has a large distance between its opposite sides or surfaces.

толстый

thick, fat

тонкий | tónkiy

Part of speech: adjective

Thin, as in "The paper is very **thin**" (Бумага очень **тонкая**.). It is an adjective used to describe something that has a small distance between its opposite sides or surfaces.

тонкий

thin, slender

торт | tort

Part of speech: noun

Gender: masculine

Cake, as in "She baked a chocolate **cake** for the party" (Она испекла шоколадный **торт** для вечеринки.). It is a noun used to describe a sweet baked dessert, typically made with flour, sugar, and other ingredients, and often decorated or layered.

торт

cake

точно | tóchno

Part of speech: adverb

Exactly, as in "That's **exactly** what I meant" (Это **точно** то, что я имел в виду.). It is an adverb used to confirm that something is correct or accurate.

точно

exactly, precisely

трамвай | tramváy

Part of speech: noun

Gender: masculine

Tram, as in "We took the **tram** to get to the city center" (Мы поехали на **трамвае** в центр города.). It is a noun used to describe a rail vehicle that runs on tracks along public urban streets and also sometimes on separate rights of way.

трамвай

tram, streetcar

три | tri

Part of speech: numeral

Three, as in "I have **three** books" (У меня есть **три** книги.).
It is a numeral used to represent the number 3.

три

three

триатлон | triatlón

Part of speech: noun

Gender: masculine

Triathlon, as in "He is training for a **triathlon**" (Он тренируется для участия в **триатлоне**.).
It is a noun used to describe a multi-sport race consisting of swimming, cycling, and running in immediate succession over various distances.

триатлон

triathlon

тридцать | trídtsat'

Part of speech: numeral

Thirty, as in "She is **thirty** years old" (Ей **тридцать** лет.).
It is a numeral used to represent the number 30.

тридцать

thirty

тринадцать | trinádtsat'

Part of speech: numeral

Thirteen, as in "He has **thirteen** apples" (У него **тринадцать** яблок.).
It is a numeral used to represent the number 13.

тринадцать

thirteen

триста | trísta

Part of speech: numeral

Three hundred, as in "The book costs **three hundred** rubles" (Книга стоит **триста** рублей.). It is a numeral used to represent the number 300.

триста

three hundred

трудный | trúdnıy

Part of speech: adjective

Difficult, as in "This is a **difficult** task" (Это **трудная** задача.). It is an adjective and is often used to describe something that requires a lot of effort or skill to accomplish.

трудный

difficult, hard

трудовой договор | trudovóy dogovór

Part of speech: noun phrase

Gender: masculine

Employment contract, as in "She signed an **employment contract** with the company" (Она подписала **трудовой** договор с компанией.). It is a noun phrase and is often used to describe a formal agreement between an employer and an employee outlining the terms of employment.

трудовой договор

employment contract

трудолюбивый | trudolyubívyy

Part of speech: adjective

Diligent, as in "He is a **diligent** worker" (Он **трудолюбивый** работник.). It is an adjective and is often used to describe someone who is careful and persistent in their work or duties.

трудолюбивый

diligent

туалет | tualét

Part of speech: noun

Gender: masculine

Toilet, as in "Where is the **toilet**?" (Где находится **туалет**?). It is a noun and is often used to refer to a room or facility equipped with a toilet and sometimes a sink.

туалет

toilet, restroom

туман | tumán

Part of speech: noun

Gender: masculine

Fog, as in "The city was covered in **fog**" (Город был покрыт **туманом**.). It is a noun and is often used to describe a thick cloud of tiny water droplets suspended in the atmosphere, reducing visibility.

туман

fog, mist

туманно | tumánno

Part of speech: adverb

Foggy, as in "It is **foggy** outside today" (Сегодня на улице **туманно**.). It is an adverb and is often used to describe weather conditions where there is a lot of fog, reducing visibility.

туманно

foggy, misty

туннель | tunnél'

Part of speech: noun

Gender: masculine

Tunnel, as in "The train passed through the **tunnel**" (Поезд прошёл через **туннель**.). It is a noun and is often used to describe an underground or underwater passage, typically for vehicles or trains.

туннель

tunnel

турист | tourist

Part of speech: noun

Gender: masculine

Tourist, as in "The **tourist** visited many famous landmarks" (**Турист** посетил много известных достопримечательностей.). It is a noun and is often used to describe a person who is traveling or visiting a place for pleasure.

турист

tourist

туристическое агентство | uristícheskoye agéntstvo

Part of speech: noun phrase

Gender: neuter

Travel Agency, as in "We booked our vacation through a **travel agency**" (Мы забронировали наш отпуск через **туристическое агентство**.). It is a noun phrase used to describe a business that arranges travel and accommodation for travelers.

туристическое агентство

travel agency

ты | ty

Part of speech: pronoun

You, as in "How are **you**?" (Как **ты**?). It is a pronoun and is often used in informal contexts to address a single person, typically someone you know well, such as a friend or family member.

ты

you

тысяча | tysjácha

Part of speech: noun

Gender: feminine

Thousand, as in "There are a **thousand** stars in the sky" (На небе **тысяча** звёзд.). It is a noun and is often used to describe a large number.

тысяча

thousand

тяжело | teželó

Part of speech: adverb

Heavily, as in "He breathed **heavily** after the run" (Он **тяжело** дышал после пробежки.). It is an adverb and is often used to describe the manner of an action.

тяжело

heavily, hard

тяжелый | teželý

Part of speech: adjective

Heavy, as in "The box is too **heavy** to lift" (Коробка слишком **тяжелая**, чтобы её поднять.). It is an adjective and is often used to describe something with a lot of weight.

тяжелый

heavy

тянуть | tinút' (Imperfective)

Part of speech: verb
Verb group: -уть

Perfective: потянуть | potinút'

To pull, as in "He tried **to pull** the rope" (Он пытался **тянуть** верёвку.). It is a verb and is often used to describe the action of exerting force to move something towards oneself.

тянуть

to pull

увольнение | uvol'nénie

Part of speech: noun

Gender: neuter

Dismissal, as in "The company announced the **dismissal** of several employees" (Компания объявила об **увольнении** нескольких сотрудников.). It is a noun and is often used to describe the act of terminating someone's employment.

увольнение

dismissal, layoff

угловатый | uglovátý

Part of speech: adjective

Angular, as in "The sculpture had an **angular** design" (Скульптура имела **угловатый** дизайн.). It is an adjective and is often used to describe something with sharp angles or a geometric appearance.

угловатый

angular

удостоверение личности | udostoverénie líchnosti

Part of speech: noun phrase

Gender: neuter

Identity card, as in "You need to show your **identity card** at the entrance" (Вам нужно показать **удостоверение личности** на входе.). It is a noun phrase used to refer to an official document that verifies a person's identity.

удостоверение личности

to run

уже | užé

Part of speech: adverb

Already, as in "She has **already** finished her homework" (Она **уже** закончила домашнее задание.). It is an adverb used to indicate that something has happened before the present time or earlier than expected.

уже

already

ужин | úzhin

Part of speech: noun

Gender: masculine

Dinner, as in "We are having **dinner** at 7 PM" (Мы **ужинаем** в 7 вечера.).
It is a noun used to refer to the main meal of the evening.

ужин

dinner

узкий | úzkij

Part of speech: adjective

Narrow, as in "The street is too **narrow** for large vehicles" (Улица слишком
узкая для больших транспортных средств.). It is an adjective used to
describe something that has a small width or is limited in space.

узкий

narrow

укачивание | ukáchivanie

Part of speech: noun

Gender: neuter

Motion sickness, as in "She often experiences **motion sickness** during long car rides" (Она часто
испытывает **укачивание** во время длительных поездок на машине.). It can also refer to
the act of rocking, such as soothing a baby to sleep.

укачивание

motion sickness

уксус | úksus

Part of speech: noun

Gender: masculine

Vinegar, as in "Add a tablespoon of **vinegar** to the salad dressing" (Добавьте столовую ложку
уксуса в заправку для салата.). It is a noun used to refer to a sour liquid used in cooking and
food preservation.

уксус

vinegar

улица | úlitsa

Part of speech: noun

Gender: masculine

Street, as in "The children are playing on the **street**" (Дети играют на **улице**.). It is a noun used to refer to a public road in a city or town, typically with buildings on one or both sides.

улица

street

умирать | umirát' (Imperfective)

Part of speech: verb
Verb group: -ать

Perfective: умереть | umerét'

Die, as in "The plant will **die** without water" (Растение **умрёт** без воды.). It is a verb and is often used to describe the process of ceasing to live or the end of life.

умирать

to die

умный | úmnyy

Part of speech: adjective

Smart, as in "She is a **smart** student" (Она **умная** студентка.). It is an adjective and is often used to describe someone who is intelligent or quick-witted.

умный

smart, intelligent

университет | universitét

Part of speech: noun

Gender: masculine

University, as in "He studies at the **university**" (Он учится в **университете**.). It is a noun and is often used to refer to an institution of higher education and research.

университет

university

уродливый | uródlivyy

Part of speech: adjective

Ugly, as in "The building is **ugly** but functional" (Здание **уродливое**, но функциональное.).
It is an adjective and is often used to describe something that is unpleasant to look at.

уродливый

ugly

усталый | ustályy

Part of speech: adjective

Tired, as in "She felt **tired** after the long journey" (Она чувствовала себя **усталой** после долгого путешествия.). It is an adjective and is often used to describe a state of fatigue or exhaustion.

усталый

tired

усы | usý

Part of speech: noun

Gender: masculine

Mustache, as in "He decided to grow a **mustache**" (Он решил отрастить **усы**.).
It is a noun and is often used to describe facial hair above the upper lip.

усы

mustache

утро | útro

Part of speech: noun

Gender: neuter

Morning, as in "The **morning** was bright and sunny" (**Утро** было ярким и солнечным.). It is a noun and is often used to describe the early part of the day.

утро

morning

ухо | úkho

Part of speech: noun

Gender: neuter

Ear, as in "She whispered in his **ear**" (Она прошептала ему на **ухо**.).
It is a noun and is often used to describe the organ of hearing.

ухо

ear

учитель | uchítel'

Part of speech: noun

Gender: masculine

Teacher, as in "The **teacher** explained the lesson clearly" (**Учитель** ясно объяснил урок.).
It is a noun and is often used to describe someone who instructs or educates students.

учитель

teacher

учить | uchít' (Imperfective)

Part of speech: verb
Verb group: -ить

Perfective: выучить | výuchít'

Learn, as in "He **learns** Russian every day" (Он **учит** русский язык каждый день.).
It is a verb and is often used to describe the process of acquiring knowledge or skills.

учить

to learn

фрукты | frúkty

Part of speech: noun

Gender: masculine

Fruits, as in "She bought fresh **fruits** at the market" (Она купила свежие **фрукты** на рынке.).
It is a noun and is often used to refer to edible sweet and fleshy products of a tree or other plant.

фрукты

fruits

футбол | futból

Part of speech: noun

Gender: masculine

Football, as in "He plays **football** every weekend" (Он играет в **футбол** каждые выходные.). It is a noun and is often used to refer to the sport played between two teams of eleven players with a round ball that may not be touched with the hands or arms during play, except by the goalkeepers.

футбол

football, soccer

хлеб | khleb

Part of speech: noun

Gender: masculine

Bread, as in "She bought fresh **bread** from the bakery" (Она купила свежий **хлеб** в пекарне.).
It is a noun and is often used to refer to a staple food made from flour and water, usually by baking.

хлеб

bread

хоккей на льду | khokkéy na l'dú

Part of speech: noun phrase

Gender: masculine

ice hockey, as in "**Ice hockey** is a popular sport in Canada" (**Хоккей на льду** — популярный спорт в Канаде.). It is a noun phrase and is often used to refer to the fast-paced team sport played on ice, where skaters use sticks to direct a puck into the opposing team's goal.

хоккей на льду

ice hockey

холодный | kholódnyy

Part of speech: adjective

Cold, as in "The water is very **cold**" (Вода очень **холодная**.). It is an adjective and is often used to describe a low temperature or a lack of warmth.

холодный

cold

хороший | khoróshiy

Part of speech: adjective

Good, as in "He is a **good** friend" (Он **хороший** друг.). It is an adjective and is often used to describe something of high quality or that is favorable or satisfactory.

хороший

good

хорошо | khoroshó

Part of speech: adverb

Well, as in "She sings **well**" (Она **хорошо** поёт.). It is an adverb and is often used to describe the manner in which an action is performed, indicating a high quality or satisfactory level.

хорошо

well

хотеть | khotét' (Imperfective)

Perfective: захотеть | zakhotét'

Part of speech: verb
Verb group: irregular

To want, as in "I **want** to eat" (Я **хочу** есть.). It is a verb used to express a desire or wish for something.

хотеть

to want

хотя | khotyá

Part of speech: conjunction

Although, as in "**Although** it was raining, we went for a walk." (**Хотя** шёл дождь, мы пошли на прогулку.). It is a conjunction and is often used to introduce a contrast or exception.

хотя

although

храбрый | khrábrıy

Part of speech: adjective

Brave, as in "The **brave** soldier faced the enemy." (**Храбрый** солдат встретил врага.).
It is an adjective and is often used to describe someone who shows courage.

храбрый

brave

хуже | khúzhe

Part of speech: adverb

Worse, as in "The weather today is **worse** than yesterday." (Погода сегодня **хуже**, чем вчера.).
It is an adverb and is often used to compare the quality or condition of something unfavorably.

хуже

worse

цветок | tsvetók

Gender: masculine

Part of speech: noun

Flower, as in "The **flower** bloomed beautifully in the garden." (**Цветок** красиво
расцвёл в саду.). It is a noun and is often used to refer to a plant or blossom.

цветок

flower

церковь | tsérkov'

Gender: masculine

Part of speech: noun

Church, as in "The **church** is located in the center of the town." (**Церковь** находится в центре
города.). It is a noun and is often used to refer to a building used for public Christian worship.

церковь

church

чаевые | chayevýe

Part of speech: noun

Gender: plural

Tips, as in "We left a generous **tip** for the waiter." (Мы оставили щедрые **чаевые** официанту.).
It is a noun and is often used to refer to money given to service workers for their services.

чаевые

tips

чай | cháy

Part of speech: noun

Gender: masculine

Tea, as in "I drink **tea** every morning." (Я пью **чай** каждое утро.). It is a noun and
is often used to refer to the beverage made by infusing dried leaves in boiling water.

чай

tea

час | chas

Part of speech: noun

Gender: masculine

Hour, as in "The meeting will last for one **hour**." (Встреча продлится
один **час**.). It is a noun and is often used to refer to a

час

hour

часто | chásto

Part of speech: adverb

Often, as in "She **often** visits her grandparents." (Она **часто** навещает своих бабушку и
дедушку.). It is an adverb and is used to describe something that happens frequently or regularly.

часто

often

чашка | cháshka

Part of speech: noun

Gender: feminine

Cup, as in "I drank a **cup** of coffee this morning." (Я выпил **чашку** кофе этим утром.). It is a noun and is often used to refer to a small, typically cylindrical container used for drinking beverages.

чашка

cup

чей | chey

Part of speech: pronoun

Whose, as in "**Whose** book is this?" (**Чья** это книга?).
It is a pronoun used to ask about ownership or possession.

чей

whose

челюсть | chélyust'

Part of speech: noun

Gender: feminine

Jaw, as in "He has a strong **jaw**." (У него крепкая **челюсть**.). It is a noun and is often used to refer to the lower part of the face that moves when you open your mouth.

челюсть

jaw

чемодан | chemodán

Part of speech: noun

Gender: masculine

suitcase, as in "I packed my **suitcase** for the trip." (Я упаковал свой **чемодан** для поездки.).
It is a noun and is often used to refer to a large, rectangular bag or case used for carrying clothes and other personal belongings when traveling.

чемодан

suitcase

через | chérez

Part of speech: preposition

Across, as in "We walked **across** the bridge." (Мы прошли **через** мост.). It is a preposition used to indicate movement from one side to the other side of something.

через

across

через пять минут | chérez pyat' minut

Part of speech: prepositional phrase

In five minutes, as in "The meeting will start **in five minutes**." (Встреча начнется **через пять минут**.). This phrase is used to indicate that something will happen after a period of five minutes from the current time.

через пять минут

in five minutes

четверг | chetverg

Part of speech: noun

Gender: masculine

Thursday, as in "We have a meeting on **Thursday**." (У нас встреча в **четверг**.). It is a noun used to refer to the fifth day of the week in many calendars, following Wednesday and preceding Friday.

четверг

Thursday

четыре | chetýre

Part of speech: numeral

Four, as in "I have **four** books." (У меня есть **четыре** книги.).
It is a numeral used to represent the quantity or number 4.

четыре

four

четыреста | chetýresta

Four hundred, as in "The book costs **four hundred** rubles." (Книга стоит **четыреста** рублей.). It is a numeral used to represent the quantity or number 400.

четыреста

four hundred

четырнадцать | chetýrnadtsat'

Fourteen, as in "She is **fourteen** years old." (Ей **четырнадцать** лет.).
It is a numeral used to represent the quantity or number 14.

четырнадцать

fourteen

чистый | chístyy

Clean, as in "The room is **clean**." (Комната **чистая**.). It is an adjective used to describe something that is free from dirt, marks, or stains.

чистый

clean

читать | chitat'

Perfective: прочитать | prochitat'

To read, as in "I like **to read** books." (Я люблю **читать** книги.). It is a verb used to describe the action of looking at and comprehending the meaning of written or printed matter.

читать

to read

что | chto

Part of speech: pronoun

What, as in "**What** is this?" (**Что** это?). It is a pronoun used to ask questions about things or to refer to something previously mentioned.

что

what

что-то | chto-to

Part of speech: pronoun

Something, as in "I heard **something**." (Я слышал **что-то**.).
It is a pronoun used to refer to an unspecified or unknown thing.

что-то

something

чувствовать | chuvstvovat' (Imperfective)

Part of speech: verb
Verb group: -овать
special subgroup of the -ать verb group

Perfective: почувствовать | pochúvstvovat'

Feel, as in "I **feel** happy today." (Я **чувствую** себя счастливым сегодня.). It is a verb and is often used to describe experiencing emotions or physical sensations.

чувствовать

to feel

шахматы | shákhmaty

Part of speech: noun
Gender: plural

Chess, as in "We play **chess** every weekend." (Мы играем в **шахматы** каждые выходные.).
It is a noun and is often used to refer to the board game involving strategic moves.

шахматы

chess

шептать | sheptát' (Imperfective)

Part of speech: verb
Verb group: -ать

Perfective: прошептать | прошептать

Whisper, as in "She likes **to whisper** secrets." (Она любит **шептать** секреты.).
It is a verb and is often used to describe speaking very quietly.

шептать

to whisper

шестнадцать | shestnádtsat'

Part of speech: numeral

Sixteen, as in "He is **sixteen** years old." (Ему **шестнадцать** лет.).
It is a numeral and is often used to denote the number sixteen.

шестнадцать

sixteen

шесть | shést'

Part of speech: numeral

Six, as in "There are **six** apples on the table." (На столе **шесть** яблок.).
It is a numeral and is often used to denote the number six.

шесть

six

шестьдесят | shest'desyát

Part of speech: numeral

sixty, as in "The book costs **sixty** rubles." (Книга стоит **шестьдесят** рублей.).
It is a numeral and is often used to denote the number sixty.

шестьдесят

sixty

шестьсот | shest'sót

Part of speech: numeral

Six hundred, as in "The library has **six hundred** books." (В библиотеке **шестьсот** книг.).
It is a numeral and is often used to denote the number six hundred.

шестьсот

six hundred

шея | shéya
Gender: feminine

Part of speech: noun

Neck, as in "He wore a scarf around his **neck**." (Он носил шарф вокруг **шеи**.). It is a noun
and is often used to refer to the part of the body connecting the head to the rest of the body.

шея

neck

широкий | shirókiy

Part of speech: adjective

Wide, as in "The river is very **wide**." (Река очень **широкая**.). It is an adjective
used to describe something that has a considerable or great extent from side to side.

широкий

wide, broad

школа | shkóla
Gender: feminine

Part of speech: noun

School, as in "She goes to **school** every day." (Она ходит в **школу** каждый день.). It is a noun
used to refer to an institution for educating children or a place where learning takes place.

школа

school

шоколад | shokolád

Part of speech: noun

Gender: masculine

Chocolate, as in "I love eating **chocolate**." (Я люблю есть **шоколад**.). It is a noun used to refer to a sweet, brown food made from roasted and ground cacao seeds, typically sweetened and eaten as a confection or used as a flavoring ingredient in other foods.

шоколад

chocolate

шоссе | shossé

Part of speech: noun

Gender: neuter

Highway, as in "The **highway** was busy with traffic" (**Шоссе** было загружено транспортом.).
It is a noun and is often used to refer to a major road designed for fast traffic.

шоссе

highway, road

шторм | shtorm

Part of speech: noun

Gender: masculine

Storm, as in "The ship was caught in a **storm**." (Корабль попал в **шторм**.). It is a noun used to describe a violent disturbance of the atmosphere with strong winds and usually rain, thunder, lightning, or snow.

шторм

storm

щека | shcheká

Part of speech: noun

Gender: feminine

Cheek, as in "She kissed him on the **cheek**." (Она поцеловала его в **щеку**.). It is a noun used to refer to the fleshy part of the face below the eye and between the nose and the ear.

щека

cheek

экскурсия по городу | ekskúrsiya po górodu
Part of speech: noun phrase

Gender: feminine

City tour, as in "We went on a **city tour** to see the main attractions." (Мы отправились на **экскурсию по городу**, чтобы увидеть главные достопримечательности.). This phrase is used to describe a guided visit around a city, often highlighting important landmarks and attractions.

экскурсия по городу

city tour

электрик | elektrík
Part of speech: noun

Gender: masculine

Electrician, as in "The **electrician** fixed the wiring." (**Электрик** починил проводку.).
It is a noun used to refer to a person who installs and maintains electrical equipment.

электрик

electrician

электричество | elektríchestvo
Part of speech: noun

Gender: neuter

Electricity, as in "The **electricity** went out during the storm." (**Электричество** отключилось во время шторма.). It is a noun used to refer to the form of energy resulting from the existence of charged particles.

электричество

electricity

это | éto
Part of speech: pronoun

This, as in "**This** is a book." (**Это** книга.). It is a pronoun and is often used to refer to something that is close to the speaker or to introduce something.

это

this, it

Это далеко? | Éto dalekó?

Part of speech: phrase

Is it far?, as in "**Is it far**?" (**Это далеко**?). It is a phrase used to inquire about the distance to a particular location.

Это далеко?

Is it far?

Я | ya

Part of speech: pronoun

I, as in "**I** am happy" (**Я** счастлив.).
It is a pronoun and is often used to refer to oneself.

Я

I

яблоко | yábloko

Part of speech: noun

Gender: neuter

Apple, as in "I ate an **apple**" (Я съел **яблоко**.).
It is a noun and is often used to refer to the fruit.

яблоко

apple

язык | yazýk

Part of speech: noun

Gender: masculine

Tongue, as in "He burned his **tongue** on the hot soup" (Он обжёг **язык** горячим супом.). It is a noun and is often used to refer to the muscular organ in the mouth.

язык

tongue

3
Flashcards

On the next 90 pages you will find a total of 720 flashcards that you can cut out and use to learn. According to the learning strategy in this book, you should learn 8, 16 or 24 new words every day, depending on how much time you can spare. This means that you cut out new vocabulary every day and then learn with it.

The cards are sorted by relevance. So you don't learn alphabetically, but according to our learning sequence created especially for this book. This means that the vocabulary is related to each other and you don't just learn random words, but in an intelligent order so that you learn with maximum effectiveness.

As already mentioned, you can also use the QR code at the bottom of this page to download all the cards as a PDF, print them out and make as many new cards as you like. This was so important to me so that you always have a replacement if you lose a card or one breaks. The old version of the book was sorted alphabetically, the current one has the new learning order. Below you will find PDFs to print out both.

As an alternative or in addition to the cut-out flashcards, you can use Quizlet to learn all the flashcards online. Quizlet has the great advantage that you learn the correct pronunciation directly, as Quizlet can read the Russian words to you. So I would definitely recommend that you learn at least part of the language with Quizlet.

If you have any questions, you can always contact me by e-mail (russisch@selbstgelernt.com) and I will be happy to help you where I can. Sometimes it may take me a few days to answer, but I will definitely reply!

Also, if you like the book, I'd love to see a review on Amazon! Maybe even with a photo of the book, that would support me the most. Just go to your Amazon orders and write a review. But now, above all, I wish you every success in learning with this book!

PDF sorted
alphabetically

PDF with effective
learning order

this, it	evening
you	work, job
ATM	tree
sorry	please
he	flower
food	book
family	bus
window	thank you

вечер	это
работа	ты
дерево	банкомат
пожалуйста	извините извинить
цветок	он
книга	еда
автобус	семья
спасибо	окно

I	airplane
you (plural)	woman
yes	friend
cat	money
nothing	hello
child	house
life	help, assistance
love	dog

самолёт	я
женщина	вы
друг	да
деньги	кошка
привет	ничего
дом	ребёнок
помощь	жизнь
собака	любовь

day	man
table	night
bye	no
door	school
bird	she
water	they
we	street
time	chair

мужчина	день
ночь	стол
нет	пока
школа	дверь
она	птица
они	вода
улица	мы
стул	время

to need	train
to thank	mobile phone
to think	to start, to begin
to end	to answer, to reply
to explain	to work
to eat	to build
to go	to use
to find	to stay

поезд	нуждаться потребовать
мобильный телефон	благодарить поблагодарить
начинать начать	думать подумать
отвечать ответить	заканчивать закончить
работать поработать	объяснять объяснить
строить построить	есть съесть
использовать (imperfective & perfective)	ехать поехать
оставаться остаться	находить найти

to have	to cost
to win	to come
to go	to cook
to give	to buy
to feel	to hear
to ask	to hope
to whisper	to help
to fly	to marry

летать полететь	жениться пожениться
шептать прошептать	помогать помочь
спрашивать спросить	надеяться понадеяться
чувствовать почувствовать	слышать услышать
давать дать	покупать купить
идти пойти	готовить приготовить
побеждать победить	приходить прийти
иметь получить	стоить

to open	to laugh
to try	to live
to travel	to teach
to run	to learn
to repair	to read
to call	to love, to like
to say, to tell	to do, to make
to send, to dispatch	to take

смеяться засмеяться	открывать открыть
жить прожить	пробовать попробовать
преподавать преподать	путешествовать попутешествовать
учить выучить	бежать побежать
читать прочитать	ремонтировать отремонтировать
любить полюбить	звонить позвонить
делать сделать	сказать говорить сказать is the perfective verb here
брать взять	отправлять отправить

to be	to search
to see	to die
to swim	to stand
to shout, to scream	to jump
to write	to speak, to talk
to close	to play
to sleep	to sit
to push	to remember

толкать толкнуть	помнить запомнить
спать поспать	сидеть сесть
закрывать закрыть	играть сыграть
писать написать	говорить сказать
кричать крикнуть	прыгать прыгнуть
плавать поплавать	стоять постоять
видеть увидеть	умирать умереть
быть	искать найти

to understand	to dance
to wait	to carry
to wash	to drink
to cry	to earn
to know	to forgive
to want	to forget
to pay	to sell
to draw	to lose

танцевать потанцевать	понимать понять
нести понести	ждать побежать
пить выпить	мыть помыть
зарабатывать заработать	плакать заплакать
прощать простить	знать узнать
забывать забыть	хотеть побежать
продавать продать	платить заплатить
терять потерять	рисовать нарисоват

cheap	to show
bitter	to destroy
angry	to pull
wide, broad	old
thick, fat	old-fashioned
stupid, foolish	afraid
thin, slender	poor
thirsty, eager	busy

показывать показать	дешевый
разрушать разрушить	горький
тянуть потянуть	злой
старый	широкий
старомодный	толстый
испуганный	глупый
бедный	тонкий
занятой	жаждущий

friendly	angular
dangerous	easy
healthy	narrow
happy	incorrect, wrong
big	lazy
good	shallow
hard, solid	diligent
ugly	free

угловатый	дружелюбный
простой	опасный
узкий	здоровый
неправильный	счастливый
ленивый	большой
мелкий	хороший
трудолюбивый	твёрдый
свободный	уродливый

long	hot
slow	hungry
boring, dull	interesting
loud	young
light, easy	cold
quiet, silent	small, little
modern	sick
tired	short

горячий	длинный
голодный	медленный
интересный	скучный
молодой	громкий
холодный	лёгкий
маленький	тихий
больной	современный
короткий	усталый

clean	new
sour	curious
smart, intelligent	embarrassing
bad	punctual
dirty	rich
fast, quick	right
beautiful	round
shy, timid	salty

новый	чистый
любопытный	кислый
неловкий	умный
пунктуальный	плохой
богатый	грязный
правильный	быстрый
круглый	красивый
соленый	застенчивый

sad	heavy
unfriendly	difficult, hard
unpunctual, tardy	safe
unimportant	proud
careful, cautious	sweet
awake	brave
warm	expensive
soft	deep

тяжелый	грустный
трудный	недружелюбный
безопасный	непунктуальный
гордый	неважный
сладкий	осторожный
храбрый	бодрый
дорогой	теплый
глубокий	мягкий

inside	important
almost	deliberately
earlier, before	differently
exactly, precisely	soon
separately, apart	especially
usually	better
immediately, soon	there
well	outside

важный	внутри
намеренно	почти
иначе	раньше
скоро	точно
особенно	отдельно
лучше	обычно
там	сразу
снаружи	хорошо

sometimes	mainly, mostly
of course, certainly	here
never	always
nowhere	somewhere
not yet	now
normally	barely
above, upstairs	slowly
often	easily

в основном	иногда
здесь	конечно
всегда	никогда
где-то	нигде
сейчас	ещё не
едва	нормально
медленно	наверху
легко	часто

immediately	suddenly
later	badly, poorly
actually, in fact	worse
everywhere	quickly, fast
necessarily, definitely	already
below	heavily, hard
maybe, perhaps	rarely
probably	surely, certainly

вдруг	немедленно
плохо	позже
хуже	на самом деле
быстро	везде
уже	обязательно
тяжело	внизу
редко	может быть
наверняка	вероятно

admission ticket	really, truly
ferry	by chance, accidentally
travel ticket	together
airport	adventure
guide	car
currency exchange	mountain
luggage	bus stop
border	village

действительно	входной билет
случайно	паром
вместе	проездной билет
приключение	аэропорт
машина	гид
гора	обмен валюты
автобусная остановка	багаж
деревня	граница

ocean	border control
passenger	hotel
postcard, greeting card	island
trip, journey	camera
travel agency	suitcase
guidebook	country
motion sickness	sea
passport	rented car

пограничный контроль	океан
гостиница	пассажир
остров	открытка
камера	поездка
чемодан	туристическое агентство
страна	путеводитель
море	укачивание
арендованный автомобиль	паспорт

city	travel bag
city tour	destination
beach	backpack
valley	ship
taxi	attraction, landmark
ticket	security, safety
tourist	sunglasses
accommodation	souvenir

дорожная сумка	город
пункт назначения	экскурсия по городу
рюкзак	пляж
корабль	долина
достопримечательность	такси
безопасность	билет
солнечные очки	турист
сувенир	жильё

bar	dessert
banana	cocktail
apple	café
dinner	butter
room	bread
visa	beer
insurance	order
vacation, leave	to order

отпуск	заказывать заказать
страховка	заказ
виза	пиво
комната	хлеб
ужин	сливочное масло
яблоко	кафе
банан	коктейль
бар	десерт

vegetables	ice cream
drink, beverage	strawberry
glass	vinegar
main course	fish
chicken	meat
coffee	breakfast
potato	fork
cheese	guest

мороженое	овощи
клубника	напиток
уксус	стакан
рыба	основное блюдо
мясо	курица
завтрак	кофе
вилка	картофель
гость	сыр

milk	waiter
lunch	waitress
noodles	chef, cook
fruits	kitchen
oil	cake
orange	spoon
pasta	menu
pepper	knife

официант	молоко
официантка	обед
повар	лапша
кухня	фрукты
торт	масло
ложка	апельсин
меню	паста
нож	перец

chocolate	pizza
bowl	bill
pork	rice
napkin	restaurant
sparkling water	beef
still water	juice
straw	salad
soup	salt

пицца	шоколад
счет	миска
рис	свинина
ресторан	салфетка
говядина	газированная вода
сок	негазированная вода
салат	соломинка
соль	суп

arm	cup
eye	tea
beard	plate
stomach, belly	tips
leg	appetizer, snack
blood	wine
chest, breast	sausage
intestine	sugar

чашка	рука
чай	глаз
тарелка	борода
чаевые	живот
закуска	нога
вино	кровь
колбаса	грудь
сахар	кишечник

brush	thumb
wrist	elbow
skin, leather	finger
heart	foot
hip	brain
jaw	face
chin	hair
knee	neck

большой палец	кисть
локоть	запястье
палец	кожа
ступня	сердце
мозг	бедро
лицо	челюсть
волос	подбородок
шея	колено

muscle	ankle
nose	bone
nerves	head
ear	body
back	liver
mustache	lung
shoulder	stomach (organ)
forehead	mouth

лодыжка	мышца
кость	нос
голова	нервы
тело	ухо
печень	спина
лёгкое	усы
желудок	плечо
рот	лоб

someone, somebody	cheek
some	tooth
no one, nobody	toe
to turn	tongue
traffic light	all, everyone
exit	several, a few
highway, road	something
up to	every

щека	кто-то
зуб	некоторые
палец ноги	никто
язык	поворачивать повернуть
все	светофор
несколько	выезд
что-то	шоссе
каждый	до

in five minutes	to the south
nearby	to the east
behind, for	to the north
stop (bus, tram)	to the left
straight ahead	intersection
opposite	roundabout
entrance (for cars)	map
bridge	Is it far?

мост	Это далеко?
въезд	карта
напротив	кольцо
прямо	перекрёсток
остановка	налево
за	на север
поблизости	на восток
через пять минут	на юг

across	to the west
in front of	next to, near
past	to the right
How do I get to...?	direction
How far is it?	city map
crosswalk	tram, streetcar
on foot	tunnel
between	subway, metro

на запад	через
рядом	перед
направо	мимо
направление	Как мне добраться до...?
план города	Как далеко это
трамвай	пешеходный переход
туннель	пешком
метро	между

profession	employer
application	employee, worker
job interview	workplace
accountant	employment contract
office	doctor
boss, supervisor	baker
designer	builder
electrician	promotion

работодатель	профессия
работник	заявление
рабочее место	собеседование
трудовой договор	бухгалтер
врач	офис
пекарь	начальник
строитель	дизайнер
повышение	электрик

IT specialist	teacher
engineer	résumé
craftsman, artisan	dismissal, layoff
salary, wages	sick leave
gardener	nurse
hairdresser, barber	colleague
company	plumber
driver	side job

водитель	подработка
компания	сантехник
парикмахер	коллега
садовник	медсестра
зарплата	больничный лист
ремесленник	увольнение
инженер	резюме
айти-специалист	учитель

secretary	painter
team	manager
part-time	bricklayer, mason
translator	mechanic
overtime work	employee
business	police officer
salesperson	lawyer
contract	carpenter

маляр	секретарь
менеджер	команда
каменщик	неполный рабочий день
механик	переводчик
сотрудник	сверхурочная работа
полицейский	предприятие
адвокат	продавец
плотник	контракт

running	full-time
athletics	basketball
marathon	boxing
motorsport	ice hockey
bicycle	football, soccer
horse riding	golf
wrestling	handball
sailing	rock climbing

полный рабочий день	бег
баскетбол	лёгкая атлетика
бокс	марафон
хоккей на льду	автоспорт
футбол	велосипед
гольф	верховая езда
гандбол	борьба
скалолазание	парусный спорт

triathlon	skiing
swimming	snowboarding
chess	surfing
Tuesday	diving
this week	tennis
Thursday	table tennis, ping pong
holiday, celebration	volleyball
Friday	hike

лыжный спорт	триатлон
сноубординг	плавание
сёрфинг	шахматы
дайвинг	вторник
теннис	на этой неделе
настольный теннис	четверг
волейбол	праздник
поход	пятница

season	spring
century	spring day
decade	yesterday
last year	last night
minute	autumn
noon	autumn day
midnight	today
Wednesday	year

весна	время года
весенний день	век
вчера	десятилетие
вчера вечером	в прошлом году
осень	минута
осенний день	полдень
сегодня	полночь
год	среда

summer	month
summer day	Monday
dawn	tomorrow
sunset	morning
Sunday	in the afternoon
hour	next year
day after tomorrow	Saturday
day before yesterday	second

месяц	лето
понедельник	летний день
завтра	рассвет
утро	закат
после полудня	воскресенье
в следующем году	час
суббота	послезавтра
секунда	позавчера

lightning	fog, mist
cloudy	cool
weekend	hail
week	degree
winter day	thunderstorm
winter	to freeze
weekday	humid
forenoon	thunder

до полудня	гром
будний день	влажно
зима	замерзать замёрзнуть
зимний день	гроза
неделя	градус
выходные	град
облачно	прохладно
молния	туман

storm	foggy, misty
stormy, violently	rain
to melt, to thaw	to rain / It is raining
temperature	rainy
dryly	snow
weather	to snow / It is snowing
weather forecast	sun
wind	sunny

туманно	шторм
дождь	бурно
идёт дождь дождить подождить	таять растаять
дождливо	температура
снег	сухо
идёт снег снежить поснежить	погода
солнце	прогноз погоды
солнечно	ветер

who	windy
whose	cloud
how	when
how long	why
how often	what
how much, how many	which (f.)
why	which (m.)
where	which (n.)

ветрено	кто
облако	чей
когда	как
почему	как долго
что	как часто
которая	сколько
который	зачем
которое	где

and	from where
while	where to
because	but
if	before
pharmacy	after
identity card	whether, if
train station	although
bank	or

откуда	и
куда	в то время как
но	потому что
перед тем как	если
после того как	аптека
ли	удостоверение личности
хотя	вокзал
или	банк

church	brother
hospital	bus station
market	factory
Moscow	fire
museum	building
mother	store, shop
park	capital (city)
square, area	internet

брат	церковь
автовокзал	больница
завод	рынок
огонь	Москва
здание	музей
магазин	мать
столица	парк
интернет	площадь

theater	police
daughter	post office
toilet, restroom	Saint Petersburg
university	key
father	sister
apartment	son
one	electricity
two	supermarket

полиция	театр
почта	дочь
Санкт-Петербург	туалет
ключ	университет
сестра	отец
сын	квартира
электричество	один
супермаркет	два

eleven	three
twelve	four
thirteen	five
fourteen	six
fifteen	seven
sixteen	eight
seventeen	nine
eighteen	ten

три	одиннадцать
четыре	двенадцать
пять	тринадцать
шесть	четырнадцать
семь	пятнадцать
восемь	шестнадцать
девять	шестнадцать
десять	восемнадцать

twenty-seven	nineteen
twenty-eight	twenty
twenty-nine	twenty-one
thirty	twenty-two
forty	twenty-three
fifty	twenty-four
sixty	twenty-five
seventy	twenty-six

девятнадцать	двадцать семь
двадцать	двадцать восемь
двадцать один	двадцать девять
двадцать два	тридцать
двадцать три	сорок
двадцать четыре	пятьдесят
двадцать пять	шестьдесят
двадцать шесть	семьдесят

six hundred	zero
five hundred	million
four hundred	one hundred thousand
three hundred	ten thousand
two hundred	thousand
one hundred	nine hundred
ninety	eight hundred
eighty	seven hundred

восемьдесят	семьсот
девяносто	восемьсот
сто	девятьсот
двести	тысяча
триста	десять тысяч
четыреста	сто тысяч
пятьсот	миллион
шестьсот	ноль

More books from Self-taught Russian:

www.amazon.com/dp/B0D2VY6K9Q

Scan the code or type in the link and
find out more about my workbook.

Made in the USA
Las Vegas, NV
30 December 2024

15606803R00168